LOST SECRETS

OF THE GODS

LOST SECRETS
OF THE GODS

THE LATEST EVIDENCE AND REVELATIONS ON ANCIENT ASTRONAUTS, PRECURSOR CULTURES, AND SECRET SOCIETIES

EDITED BY

MICHAEL PYE AND KIRSTEN DALLEY

New Page Books
A Division of The Career Press, Inc.
Pompton Plains, NJ

LOST SECRETS OF THE GODS
EDITED BY MICHAEL PYE AND KIRSTEN DALLEY
TYPESET BY GINA SCHENCK
Cover design by theBookDesigners
Printed in the U.S.A.

To order this title, please call toll-free 1-800-CAREER-1 (NJ and Canada: 201-848-0310) to order using VISA or MasterCard, or for further information on books from Career Press.

The Career Press, Inc.
220 West Parkway, Unit 12
Pompton Plains, NJ 07444
www.careerpress.com
www.newpagebooks.com

Library of Congress Cataloging-in-Publication Data

Lost secrets of the gods: the latest evidence and revelations on ancient astronauts, precursor cultures, and secret societies/edited by Michael Pye and Kirsten Dalley.
     pages cm
  Includes bibliographical references and index.
ISBN 978-1-60163-324-8 (paperback)--ISBN 978-1-60163-445-0 (ebook)
1. Civilization, Ancient--Extraterrestrial influences. 2. Extra-errestrial beings--History--To 1500. 3. Astronauts--History--To 1500. 4. Secret societies--History--To 1500. I. Pye, Michael, 1946- II. Dalley, Kirsten.

CB156.L67 2014
930--dc23

                                                                        2014014336

CONTENTS

Introduction:
Let's Keep Exploring

Mysteries of the past abound. How could they not?

No matter how much information is uncovered regarding the history of humanity and the larger narrative of the Earth itself, we will likely never learn the whole truth about everything that has happened on or to our world, let alone what has happened out in space, perhaps on other worlds not entirely dissimilar from our own. Even with all the evidence currently at our disposal—ancient architecture, fossil records, extant written records, oral accounts passed down through the ages—even with all this, even the most knowledgeable historians, anthropologists, and linguists know that we have barely begun to scratch the surface of humanity's origins and history. It is a seemingly never-ending quest to unravel a mystery—perhaps *the* great mystery of all time.

Given this, we decided to put together this second anthology related to ancient mysteries. This time, however, we aimed to venture a little farther afield than we did in the previous volume, *Exposed, Uncovered, and Declassified: Lost Civilizations and Secrets of the Past*. We gathered more information on the history of the Americas as well as some thought-provoking offerings on humanity's link to the cosmos. As well, we delved into some interesting theories regarding the existing world financial order, and revealed some startling similarities between what were previously thought to be unrelated cultures. Regardless of whether you accept the ancient astronaut theory or not, the ancients sure seemed to get around!

Far too much priceless information has been lost in the sands of time. With this volume we hope to have found some answers—or, at the very least, to have fomented discussion (and even rousing arguments!) that will, if the rules of discourse still stand, further the cause of knowledge. Sometimes, though, it isn't about getting the answers, but asking the right questions. Here's to asking those questions, the subversive questions that many people are too afraid to ask. Here's to exploring!

—Michael Pye and Kirsten Dalley

April 2014

Secret Societies Circa 10,000 BCE

By Robert M. Schoch, PhD

In our modern age many people are highly skeptical of, or simply dismiss, the notion of secret societies as anything more than rather childish fraternities and sororities. Furthermore, many modern so-called secret societies are not secret at all, for we know all about them. A few famous examples: Ordo Templi Orientis, the Illuminati (used loosely, with many divisions and branches), the Hermetic Order of the Golden Dawn, Skull and Bones, the Knights of Columbus, various groups of Masons and Freemasons, Rosicrucian groups, and the Bilderberg Group. Indeed, this brings up the issue of what, exactly, constitutes a secret society. To be a true secret society, should the very existence of the society be unknown to outsiders? Or might the existence, and possibly even the membership (perhaps only to a limited degree) be known, but the activities, rituals, and agenda be unknown to non-members? (Traditionally not all members will be privy to the innermost secrets and activities of the society, only those at the highest levels of initiation.) We should also make the distinction between secret societies that are conspiracy-based, where secrecy is important for political, military, and commercial scheming, and secret societies that are knowledge-based, where the knowledge, usually of an esoteric and occult nature, often includes spiritual insights and revelations deemed not fit to be revealed to the general populace. Of course these two *raisons d'être* behind forming and maintaining secret societies are not mutually exclusive. It is not uncommon for a secret society to be founded initially to guard "sacred" knowledge, but ultimately take the form of a secret conspiracy that aggrandizes through power, wealth, and status the members (or at least the top hierarchy) of the society. In this piece, my focus will be on knowledge-based secret societies.

Nowadays, it seems, the primary purpose of a so-called secret society is often not to actually pass on secret knowledge that has any profound practical value or non-trivial spiritual potency, but rather to form strong bonds between the members of the society, often stroking their egos and self-esteem. This is accomplished through rather meaningless and vapid rituals, secret signs, and the like, although modern rituals and signs may be traced back to symbols encoding deeper knowledge. Arguably, this is a recent development—that is, if it is indeed true (which may not be the case for the genuinely hush-hush secret societies, even today). In past centuries and millennia there were genuine secrets and valuable knowledge passed on to limited numbers of individuals who in some cases had to undergo strenuous mental and physical ordeals (which, if not conquered successfully, could result in death) before being admitted to either the society or to its inner circles. These were the initiates of secret societies (sometimes, but not always, known to the public or rumored to exist) and the recipients of secret knowledge of non-secret groups, such as classes of priests and hierophants, members of guilds, or adherents to religious or military orders, including, for instance, the Knights Templar and the Knights Hospitaller.

Many discussions of secret societies and secret knowledge (or lost knowledge, as it is sometimes called) take us back only to late ancient times, perhaps starting with the Hermetic traditions and the Gnostics of the first few centuries CE, and often focus on medieval and modern secret and pseudo-secret societies.[1] In this contribution I want to reach back further, much further, and suggest that secret societies date back to before the end of the last Ice Age, before circa 10,000 BCE. Furthermore, there may be some common threads, some continuity, from these early (more than 12,000 years old) secret societies and those of medieval and modern times. Before we move so far back in time, however, let us consider the dynastic Egyptians.

During the time period of about 4,700 to 3,000 years ago (roughly the time of the Old through the New Kingdoms), the ancient Egyptians accomplished amazing feats of architecture, produced incredible works of art, and possessed an intimate understanding of the natural world, as is expressed in what has come down to us of their belief systems, precise calendars (which had an astronomical basis), medical and mummification procedures, and various aspects of their daily life. In sum, the ancient Egyptians were the guardians of a prodigious knowledge. By their own admission, the dynastic Egyptians had inherited much of it from those whom they considered ancient. Yet, in a tradition that I believe stemmed from much earlier predecessors, the dynastic Egyptians kept their knowledge secret. My old friend and colleague John Anthony West—the man who convinced me to take my first trip to Egypt back in 1990, specifically to study the Great Sphinx—has discussed this at some length.

> In every field of Egyptian knowledge, the underlying principles were kept secret, but made manifest in works. If this knowledge was ever written in books—and there is mention of sacred libraries whose contents have never been found—then these books were intended only for those who had earned the right to consult them.[2]

> Beyond a certain level, in every one of the arts and sciences of Egypt, knowledge was *secret*. The rules, axioms, theorems and formulae—the very stuff of modern science and scholarship—were never made public, and may never have been written down.[3]

To the modern mind such secrecy may not even make sense. Yes, today there are some secrets, such as state or military or commercially valuable secrets, but why would a civilization keep virtually all "higher" knowledge secret? This is a supremely important question, and in some respects gets to the heart of the matter when it comes to the rationale behind secret societies in ancient times. To quote John Anthony West once again,

> But the question of secrecy is today thoroughly misunder-stood. It is generally agreed among scholars that most ancient societies (and many modern primitive ones) reserved certain types of knowledge for select initiates. At best this practice is considered absurd and undemocratic, at worst it is considered a form of intellectual tyranny, by which a class of priestly con-men kept the masses in a state of quiescent awe. But the ancient mind was rather subtler than our own. There were (and are) good reasons for keeping certain types of knowledge secret, including numbers and geometry; a Pythagorean practice that particularly arouses the ire of modern mathematicians.[4]

Among the good reasons cited by West to keep certain knowl-edge secret was that it could be put to ill effect if it fell into the wrong hands. In particular, West focuses on the example of har-mony and proportion, which can be used to manipulate the emotions and psyches of the recipients:

> [I]n ancient civilisations, a class of initiates had precise knowl-edge of harmonic laws. They knew how to manipulate them to create the precise effect they wanted. And they wrote this knowledge into architecture, art, music, paintings, rituals and incenses, producing Gothic cathedrals, vast Hindu temples, all the marvels of Egypt and many other sacred ancient works that even today, in ruins, produce a powerful effect upon us.[5]

In my assessment, the knowledge of harmonic laws was not used simply to elicit desired emotional or psychological responses, but to probe much more deeply. I believe this secret knowledge was used to engender and strengthen various types of psychical or paranormal experiences, including forms of telepathy, clairvoyance, out-of-body events, and the like. Conventional modern scholars and scientists

John Anthony West and Robert Schoch (pith helmet under his arm) with the Great Sphinx of Giza, Egypt, early 1990s. Photo courtesy of R. Schoch.

might scoff, relegating such ideas to the category of nonsense. Indeed I was once one of those scoffers, but after seriously delving into parapsychology and psychical studies,[6] I concluded that such an attitude is a mistake. I have little doubt that the ancient ancients—probably going back thousands or tens of thousands of years prior to dynastic Egypt—understood how to manipulate psychic forces and phenomena. This may have been one of the primary driving factors behind keeping certain forms of knowledge secret, and thus the establishment of secret societies with elaborate ordeals, rituals, and initiation rites for postulants.

Concerning the potential deep antiquity and precedents of ancient Egypt, dynastic Egyptians regarded their civilization as a legacy of an earlier epoch, and their chronological tables recorded a long period when Egypt was ruled by the Neters (so-called gods)[7] followed by a period when it was ruled by the Shemsu Hor ("companions of Horus" or "followers of the sun"), also spelled Shemasu Hor,[8] all before the beginning of dynastic Egypt, circa 3000 BCE. Trying to work out a chronology of this "mythological period," based on the regal years recorded in the texts, various estimates have placed the founding of Egypt between circa 30,000 BCE and 23,000 BCE.[9] The Greek historian Herodotus (fifth century BCE) was told by his Egyptian guide that Egyptian history went back so far that "the sun had twice risen where it now set, and twice set where it now rises."[10] If, as suggested by R.A. Schwaller de Lubicz, this is referring to the rising of the sun in a particular zodiacal constellation on the vernal equinox and the setting of the Sun in an opposite (180° away) zodiacal constellation on the autumnal equinox, and thus the shifting of these positions over time (precession) such that the position of the vernal equinox among the zodiacal constellations is where the autumnal equinox formerly was and vice versa, then this is an indication of precession. The full precessional cycle is approximately 26,000 years, so the guide's comment can be interpreted as referring to one and a half precessional cycles, or about 39,000 years, placing the founding of Egypt around 40,000 BCE!

Of course there is more literary evidence coming out of Egypt bearing on the deep antiquity of civilization and the knowledge these early civilizations possessed. Plato's story of Atlantis was reputedly told to Solon of Athens (circa 638–558 BCE) by an Egyptian priest, and Atlantis dated back to 10,000 BCE and earlier, being destroyed circa 9600 BCE (which is quite close to the modern estimate of circa 9700 BCE for the end of the last Ice Age).[11] The dynastic Egyptians also spoke of *Zep Tepi*, the "first time," the time of creation, the beginning of civilization, a time when the gods and men walked hand-in-hand. In modern terms, Zep Tepi apparently dates back to an era before circa 10,000 BCE.[12]

The evidence for the deep antiquity of ancient Egyptian civilization and their knowledge noted in the last two paragraphs is purely "literary" and thus does not carry much weight in many circles. In 1990, however, John Anthony West and I first developed the physical evidence, based on proven geological techniques, that the Great Sphinx of Giza—along with the pyramids, icons of dynastic Egypt—actually has its origins thousands of years prior to circa 3000 BCE. (The head of the Sphinx is not original, but a dynastic re-carving.) Initially I "conservatively" dated the proto-Sphinx (and Sphinx temple, which sits just east of the statue) to the period of circa 7000 BCE to 5000 BCE, but now, based on my continuing research over the last two and a half decades, I am comfortable with suggesting that the proto-Sphinx may even date back to the very end of the last Ice Age, circa 10,000 BCE.[13]

For a number of years the Great Sphinx, for all practical purposes, stood in isolation in terms of good evidence that civilization and sophisticated knowledge goes back to a time well prior to the period of 4000 BCE to 3000 BCE, as conventional archaeologists and prehistorians generally believed. This was troubling, and my critics certainly took advantage of the situation, taunting me to produce other evidence of extremely early yet sophisticated civilization. Only uncovered after my original work on the Great Sphinx was published,

Robert Schoch at Göbekli Tepe. Photograph by Catherine Ulissey, courtesy of R. Schoch and C. Ulissey.

we now have the magnificent site of Göbekli Tepe in southeastern Turkey, currently being excavated by Dr. Klaus Schmidt of the German Archaeological Institute. At Göbekli Tepe, immense, finely carved T-shaped limestone pillars—many in the range of 2 to 5 1/2 meters tall and weighing up to an estimated 10 tons or more— form Stonehenge-like circles. But unlike the rough-hewn megaliths of Stonehenge and many other European stone circles, the pillars of Göbekli Tepe are beautifully carved, with finely finished surfaces which in many cases are decorated with bas-reliefs of animals including foxes, boars, snakes, aurochs (wild cattle), birds, arthropods (scorpions, ants, and spiders),[14] and enigmatic symbols, among the most common of which resemble the letter H or an H turned 90 degrees on its side. Some of the pillars are anthropomorphic (resembling the human form), with arms, hands, belts, and loincloths. Sculptures in the round have also been found at Göbekli Tepe,

Overview of Göbekli Tepe. Photograph courtesy of R. Schoch and C. Ulissey.

including various animals, small statues of humans, and something that resembles a totem pole carved in stone. The level of sophistication seen at Göbekli Tepe, in my opinion, indicates that a true civilization existed here.

The real importance of Göbekli Tepe is its age. I have made the case that the circle of megalithic stones at Göbekli Tepe known as Enclosure D dates back to at least circa 10,000 BCE (that is, before the end of the last Ice Age, circa 9700 BCE).[15] Dr. Klaus Schmidt, the lead archaeologist at Göbekli Tepe, has stated he believes portions of Göbekli Tepe, as yet not fully excavated, may date back 14,000 years—circa 12,000 BCE, some 2,000 years before the end of the last Ice Age.[16]

So, civilization goes back to before the end of the last Ice Age. What does this have to do with secret societies?

During the summer of 2013 I came across a scholarly article on feasting activities and the origins of domestication among ancient peoples by Brian Hayden, professor in the archaeology department at Simon Fraser University, British Columbia. In it he speculates that Göbekli Tepe may have been the ritual center and headquarters of an ancient secret society of wealthy and elite individuals.[17] The headquarters of a secret society circa 10,000 BCE? Although I had been studying Göbekli Tepe for a number of years and knew that many researchers had referred to it as a temple, I had not thought of Göbekli Tepe specifically in the context of ancient secret societies. Professor Hayden's suggestion immediately sparked my interest, striking me as a distinct possibility. Were there really secret societies, passing down ancient knowledge, prior to the end of the last Ice Age 12,000 and more years ago? Do we have the physical evidence of such a secret society at Göbekli Tepe? What happened to the Göbekli Tepe secret society, and other secret societies, when disaster struck with the cataclysmic end of the Ice Age circa 9700 BCE?[18] Were all of their knowledge and wisdom lost? Or were fragments preserved and passed on to subsequent generations, perhaps even to the present day?

A few days after reading Hayden's paper I found myself pondering that remarkable philosopher, teacher, mystic, and seeker G.I. Gurdjieff (circa 1866–1949; there is disagreement as to the year of his birth). I was already familiar with Gurdjieff through his writings and especially through the book by his one-time disciple P.D. Ouspensky (1878–1947) with the tantalizing title *In Search of the Miraculous: Fragments of an Unknown Teaching.*[19] But the occasion that brought my thoughts back to Gurdjieff was a conference held at the Center for Symbolic Studies in Tillson, New York, over the weekend of July 27–28, 2013, in honor of none other than John Anthony West. JAW (many affectionately refer to him by his initials) had not only introduced me to the Great Sphinx back in 1990, as mentioned previously, which initiated my serious studies of ancient cultures, but being a "Gurdjieffian," JAW also introduced me to the ideas of this profound thinker. While I gave a presentation focused on the Great Sphinx and Göbekli Tepe, one of the other speakers, Jason Stern, a facilitator of Gurdjieff study groups, focused on Gurdjieff and his teachings. This got me thinking about various things Gurdjieff had written, which I had long taken as simply myth or fiction, perhaps created by Gurdjieff himself for literary and teaching purposes. Over the next couple of weeks I re-read and re-explored various aspects of Gurdjieff's assertions, wondering if maybe they did truly represent fragments of an ancient and unknown (or, at best, only partially known) teaching. Is it possible that Gurdjieff, as he himself claimed, had recovered portions of an ancient wisdom that went back thousands and thousands of years, perhaps even back to a secret society during the time of Göbekli Tepe?

The core of Gurdjieff's teachings is that most people most of the time are "asleep"—hypnotically following the routines of everyday life and what society expects of them—but through inner work it is possible to transcend this state, attaining a higher consciousness and fuller potential. Gurdjieff was seeking (and perhaps, for himself, had found) a unified system that encompassed "All and Everything" (the overarching title of his major writings), including an inherently meaningful universe and humanity's place and necessary function within that universe.

Two aspects of Gurdjieff's teachings, both of which I believe may help elucidate the meaning and purpose of Göbekli Tepe (although in my opinion Göbekli Tepe is much more than, and goes well beyond, these principles), are: 1) the concept of "objective art," and 2) Gurdjieff's ideas regarding the development of the human soul. "Objective art" is art from which everyone will receive the same information. Objective art has knowledge and wisdom encoded within it, which in turn can be reliably transmitted to observers and recipients of the art. As an example of objective art, at the July 2013 conference Jason Stern cited the Great Sphinx of Egypt. Objective art ties in with the ancient concept of symbols and the ability to hold, cognize, and transmit information, including information of an emotional, psychological, and psychical nature, without words and in a form that is more universal than any particular language. I am firmly convinced that there are things—important things—which cannot be adequately expressed or transmitted in words, or in words alone. This is an ancient truth that, I fear, has often been ignored or dismissed by many members of modern society. Some years ago I attended a conference at which one of the speakers began his presentation by stating, "If you cannot put it into words, you cannot think about it." As important as words are (after all, I am writing words now for you to read), I wholeheartedly disagree with this sentiment. We must learn to think *beyond* words.

At a deep level, a great piece of art may engender the same feelings, passions, and emotions across a broad spectrum of humanity. Art and symbolism come together, entangle, and interpenetrate. Is this one of the factors involved in the artistry of the incredible sculptures and bas-reliefs of Göbekli Tepe? I suspect that the builders and users of Göbekli Tepe were more advanced when it came to their use of art and symbolism than most of us are today. To interpret their art, we need to learn to think and feel and react the way the Göbekli Tepe people did.

According to Gurdjieff, one of the important tasks each person has during their physical lifetime here on planet Earth is the development of the soul. An eternal soul is not a birthright; rather, an integrated soul "that can withstand the force and shock of death" (to quote Jason Stern at the July 2013 conference) must be developed, a process that Gurdjieff referred to as "crystallization." Here it is worth quoting Gurdjieff, as recounted by Ouspensky:

> In order to be able to speak of any kind of future life there must be a certain crystallization, a certain fusion of man's inner qualities, a certain independence of external influences.

Stone "totem pole" from Göbekli Tepe now housed in the Museum of Şanlıurfa. Photograph courtesy of R. Schoch and C. Ulissey.

If there is anything in a man able to resist external influences, then this very thing itself may also be able to resist the death of the physical body. But think for yourselves what there is to withstand physical death in a man who faints or forgets every- thing when he cuts his finger? If there is anything in a man, it may survive; if there is nothing, then there is nothing to survive. But even if something survives, its future can be very varied. In certain cases of fuller crystallization what people call "reincarnation" may be possible after death, and, in other cases, what people call "existence on the other side." In both cases it is the continuation of life in the "astral body," or with the help of the "astral body." You know what the expression "astral body" means. But the systems with which you are ac- quainted and which use this expression state that *all men* have an "astral body." This is quite wrong. What may be called the "astral body" is obtained by means of fusion, that is, by means of terribly hard inner work and struggle. Man is not born with it. And only very few men acquire an "astral body." If it is formed it may continue to live after the death of the physical body, and it may be born again in another physical body. This is "reincarnation." If it is not re-born, then, in the course of time, it also dies; it is not immortal but it can live long after the death of the physical body.[20]

A beautiful carved stone pillar, colloquially referred to as a stone "totem pole," was found at Göbekli Tepe. From top to bottom, it shows the heads and arms of three figures, which are progressively smaller working down the sculpture (reminiscent of Russian dolls, matryoshkas, nested one within another). The heads and faces of the two uppermost figures are damaged and obscured; the uppermost head seems to have the ears and eyes of a beast, perhaps a bear—or is it a human wearing a bear pelt? The third figure is clear, and this third figure is apparently holding something in his/her hands, which vaguely looks like a pot or bowl but could possibly be a head, perhaps symbolic of a woman giving birth. Indeed, the entire sculpture can be interpreted as representing one generation giving rise to the next generation giving rise to the next generation—a lineage of ancestors and descendants. Another feature of the sculpture is two snakes, one on either side of the pillar, arising from the base of the sculpture. Snakes, who shed their skins and thus renew themselves, are often used to symbolize eternal life. Could this ancient sculpture, found at the possible headquarters of a secret society dating back more than 10,000 years, illustrate Gurdjieff's two great principles of objective art and the development, or "crystallization," of the psyche, the soul?

This concept of crystallization, of integrating the soul components, is a theme found among diverse later ancient and indigenous traditions around the world, including shamanic traditions and the ancient Egyptian concept of numerous psychic bodies or aspects of the human that must be kept together in order to ensure a continued existence beyond the physical earthly existence.[21] Gurdjieff was very clear that his teachings did not originate with him. He insisted "that the principles and methods of work for self-creation [which Gurdjieff himself followed] were known in ancient Babylon," and the various methods Gurdjieff taught to achieve the inner work were derived "from diverse sources ranging from Abyssinia [Ethiopia] to the Far East."[22]

Early in his life, Gurdjieff became convinced "that there really was 'a certain something' which people formerly knew, but that now this knowledge was quite forgotten."[23] Gurdjieff's father came from a Greek family that had settled in Turkey and then moved to Georgia; subsequently his father moved to Armenia where he married an Armenian, and his son, G.I. Gurdjieff, was born. Gurdjieff's father was an *ashokh* (bard) who, applying prodigious feats of memory, carried on the tradition of reciting stories and poems that had been passed down orally through innumerable generations. When still a young boy, in the late-19th century, Gurdjieff heard his father recite the Epic of Gilgamesh, including the portion concerning the story of a great flood. Years later Gurdjieff came across Gilgamesh in another context, as he recounts in the following passage:

> One day I read in a certain magazine an article in which it was said that there had been found among the ruins of Babylon some tablets with inscriptions which scholars were certain were no less than four thousand years old. This magazine also printed the inscriptions and the deciphered text—it was the legend of the hero Gilgamesh.
>
> When I realized that here was that same legend which I had so often heard as a child from my father, and particularly when I read in this text the twenty-first song [about the great flood] of the legend in almost the same form of exposition as in the songs and tales of my father, I experienced such an inner excitement that it was as if my whole future destiny depended on all this. And I was struck by the fact, at first inexplicable to me, that this legend had been handed down by *ashokhs* from generation to generation for thousands of years, and yet had reached our day almost unchanged.[24]

The Epic of Gilgamesh is more than 4,000 years old, and Gilgamesh as a historical figure probably dates to the first half of the third millennium BCE, perhaps circa 2700 BCE. It is true that ancient cuneiform tablets relating the Epic of Gilgamesh, and the flood story in particular, were discovered and translated in the 19th century, but it seems unlikely that Gurdjieff's father had learned the epic from modern scholars. Rather, one should contemplate the notion that the story really had been handed down by oral tradition over many millennia.

But it was not just the flood legend that Gurdjieff heard from his father:

There was another legend I had heard from my father, again about the "Flood before the Flood," which after this occurrence also acquired for me a quite particular significance.

In this legend it was said, also in verse, that long, long ago, as far back as seventy generations before the last deluge (and a generation was counted as a hundred years), when there was dry land where now is water and water where now is dry land, there existed on earth a great civilization.... The sole survivors of the earlier deluge were certain brethren of the former Imastun [wise men] Brotherhood, whose members had constituted a whole caste spread all over the earth....[25]

I find this a thought-provoking passage. Adopting the date of circa 2700 BCE for Gilgamesh, if the "Flood before the Flood" occurred 7,000 years earlier, this would place it at circa 9700 BCE, which is precisely the end of the last Ice Age and the time of the older portions of Göbekli Tepe, as well as very close to Plato's dating of the destruction of Atlantis. Is this simple coincidence? Or were the ashokhs actually recounting real events that took place at the end of the last Ice Age? A major solar plasma event could vaporize large amounts of water from glaciers, lakes, and oceans, which in turn would rain down continuously and cause widespread flooding. And what of the Imastun Brotherhood? If they were real, could one of their meeting places have been at Göbekli Tepe?

The Imastun Brotherhood is not the only very ancient secret society that Gurdjieff mentions in his writings. Gurdjieff also discusses the Sarmoung Brotherhood, "a famous esoteric school which, according to tradition, was founded in Babylon as far back as 2500 BC, and which was known to have existed somewhere in Mesopotamia up to the sixth or seventh century AD.... This school was said to have possessed great knowledge, containing the key to many secret mysteries."[26] Ultimately, Gurdjieff claimed to have visited the chief monastery of the Sarmoung Brotherhood, located at an undisclosed

Pillar with an aurochs (wild cattle), fox, and crane. Photograph courtesy of R. Schoch and C. Ulissey.

location in Central Asia.[27] The truth behind Gurdjieff's account is un-clear—is his story nothing more than a fantastical allegory? Perhaps, but it does raise the question of esoteric knowledge being passed down via a secret society over thousands and thousands of years.

Although not substantiated independently, at least to the best of my knowledge, Gurdjieff is reported to have told some of his students that various ancient mysteries and associated secret societies, including the origins of Sufism, date back to some 30,000 to 40,000 years ago.[28] This is the same time period as the reputed origin of Egyptian (or proto-Egyptian) civilization, as I've already discussed. Sufism is today commonly regarded as a branch of Islam, although the Sufis—perhaps best known for their "whirling dervishes"—have at times been harshly persecuted by other Muslims. However, Sufism may have much more ancient roots. Related to Sufism is Alevism, and this brings us back to Göbekli Tepe and the possibility that it represents a secret society that existed some 12,000 years ago.

Alevism, part of the general Islamic faith, is often described as a combination of Shia Islam with Sufi and Anatolian Sunni folk elements. Many subscribers to this faith today live in central Turkey. In the Turkish film *Gobeklitepe: The World's First Temple*, directed by Ahmet Turgut Yazman,[29] Istanbul-based author, mystic, and television host Metin Bobaroğlu is interviewed at length. Bobaroğlu (and Yazman) make comparisons between the features observed at Göbekli Tepe and Alevi beliefs and rituals. For instance, Alevism holds in reverence the concept of the 12 imams, who are viewed as aspects and reflections of the universe. Enclosure D at Göbekli Tepe contains 12 major pillars around its perimeter. The Alevi have a communal worship service known as the *cem* ritual, during which men and woman dance together (known as *semah*), whirling about in a pattern that has been interpreted as representing the movement of the planets around the sun. Could this tie in with astronomical aspects of Göbekli Tepe? There are also 12 services performed during the cem ritual. According to Bobaroğlu, the crane is an integral part of semah; there is even a dance of the cranes (*Turnalar Semah*). Cranes, or perhaps persons (shamans) dressed as cranes,[30] are found prominently carved on some of the pillars at Göbekli Tepe. Bobaroğlu[31] states that the crane is monogamous and the symbolism of the crane points to higher teachings, comparable, for instance, to Hermes or Thoth/Djhuty in Ancient Egypt, the scribe to the gods and the mediator between good and evil, often depicted in human form with the head of an ibis. The crane can represent the soul, and the evolved form of *Homo sapiens*, the gods and the goddesses. Potentially, Bobaroğlu suggests, this is the fundamental meaning of the crane symbolism at Göbekli Tepe as well, and he relates it to the concept of *Tevhid* in Islamic mysticism—the mutual oneness, the unity of God and humanity.

Pillar 43 at Göbekli Tepe with a possible vulture and various other birds, a scorpion and other animals, H symbols, and unidentified structures. Photograph courtesy of R. Schoch and C. Ulissey.

Is it really valid to compare Alevi beliefs and iconography to that which we see at Göbekli Tepe? Alevi beliefs arise in part from Islam, a religion that did not originate until the seventh century CE, more than 10,000 years after the height of Göbekli Tepe. However, Islam in general incorporates a number of earlier belief systems (as do all religions, inheriting and reusing elements of their predecessors), and the Alevi belief system in particular may include very ancient folk traditions and pre-Islamic shamanistic elements, which arguably could indeed date back to the end of the last Ice Age.

In his film Yazman does not solely stress possible "Turkish" or "Islamic" insights when it comes to the meaning of Göbekli Tepe. He also has a strong interest in Indian and Vedic culture, and thus he incorporated into his production substantial material from this perspective, including interviews with astronomer, physicist, and Vedic scholar B.G. Sidharth. Sidharth compared the 12 major pillars around the perimeter of Enclosure D with the 12 signs of the zodiac, which, he noted, may not have been recognized in exactly the same forms as they are today at the dawn of civilization. Regardless there were probably 12 zodiacal constellations even back then, and the number 12 is highly significant, whether it is the 12 biblical tribes, the 12 apostles of Jesus, the 12 months of the year, or the 12 houses of the zodiac).[32] Bobaroğlu agreed with the importance of the number 12, and the possible symbolism of the 12 zodiacal constellations represented by the 12 pillars. Sidharth also noted that on Pillar 43 the vulture could represent Cygnus (now referred to as a swan), and the scorpion could represent the constellation Scorpio (Scorpius).

Furthermore, he pointed out that the Milky Way, as seen from Earth, can be viewed as beginning near Scorpio and passing through Cygnus; in Vedic tradition this is represented by the image of a goddess riding on a swan. The "ball" on the vulture's wing Sidharth equated with the sun, and compared this very ancient image at Göbekli Tepe to images of the winged disc of the sun found in Egypt and elsewhere. Sidharth also noted the importance of the constellation Orion to many ancient peoples, in particular the Egyptians, who equated Orion with Osiris. He stated that based on his astronomical interpretations of the Vedas, the origins of Vedic civilization could go back to 10,000 bce—the period of Göbekli Tepe and the end of the last Ice Age. Indeed, he basically argued that the builders of Göbekli Tepe represent an ancient Vedic culture, something he had predicted would ultimately be found at this remote period.

Sidharth offered another important interpretation: A circle and crescent symbol found on the front (that is, the southern edge or side) of Pillar 18 below an H symbol may represent the solar disk and the crescent moon. Together, according to Sidharth, they could memorialize a solar eclipse (when the moon passes directly between the sun and earth, temporally blotting out the sun as seen from earth) that occurred circa 10,000 BCE. Furthermore this sun and moon crescent may represent the union of the divine male and female, respectively, a concept with which Bobaroğlu agreed. In later forms this became the royal crown, such as that of Hathor in Egypt, where the solar disc appears between the horns of a cow representing the moon.

Yazman and Bobaroğlu suggest that the H symbol found at Göbekli Tepe may refer to the central anthropomorphic pillars of Enclosure D coming together, holding hands, or embracing. Thus the T pillars would "embrace" here on Earth as the sun and the moon embrace in the heavens, representing the union of the male and female elements, the coming together of opposite polarities, the negative and the positive, representing the source of movement, the fountain of life, and the creation of the universe. One might object that the central T pillars of Enclosure D, while clearly anthropomorphic, both look more male than female. In fact, they may be either androgynous or hermaphroditic; in analogy, I think of the hermaphroditic figures common in Dogon art of West Africa, a tradition that may perpetuate deeply ancient beliefs and understandings, including knowledge passed down from the ancient Egyptians.[33] Also, I am reminded of a Dogon motif that in some cases forms an H shape, for instance, as seen on a wood statuette of a woman (the primordial mother?) with her arms extended to the sky.[34] On her belly, on either side of her navel, appear two small figures. The navel takes the form of a distinct circle with a dot in the center (representing the sun?), and the two figures (representing the ancestors or primordial couple of the Dogon, and hence of all humanity?) abut the outer rim of the navel on either side; thus they are linked and form a distinct H shape. Likewise, Andrew Collins has suggested that the H-shaped symbol represents twins and perhaps transition; walking between the pillars, according to Collins, participants in an ancient ritual would be at the threshold between the "here and there"; they would instantly transition, perhaps helped along by being in an altered state of consciousness induced by psychoactive drugs, drumming, chanting, or other trance-inducing techniques.[35] Collins has suggested that some of the symbolism at Göbekli Tepe could refer to people coming together, specifically in pairs of male and female, at a primordial mound. Similarly, in his film Yazman cites the ancient Sumerian concept of *Du-Ku*, a holy hill or mound or sacred mountain, where gods dwelled or congregated and from which humanity learned the arts of agriculture, animal husbandry, and weaving.[36]

Göbekli Tepe is currently an active archaeological site, with perhaps another 20 or more stone circles and other structures that have been identified using geophysical techniques but not yet been excavated. To even speculate on the meaning and use of Göbekli Tepe at this stage is arguably premature; furthermore, I have barely touched on the possibilities in this brief discussion. My point is simply that I find the notion that Göbekli Tepe represents the headquarters or ritual center of a secret society dating back 12,000 years quite compelling, although it does not exclude other meanings and uses of the site. Here we may have concrete evidence of secret knowledge that, in various forms, still survives to this day among select initiates.

Returning to Gurdjieff, I want to take note of another possible fragment of ancient knowledge, one that took a very concrete form. Gurdjieff claimed to have found, in the possession of an Armenian priest who had inherited it from his great-grandfather, an ancient parchment map of "pre-sand Egypt."[37] Gurdjieff surreptitiously made a copy of the map and traveled to Egypt, "hoping to find, with the help of my map of pre-sand Egypt, an explanation of the Sphinx and of certain other monuments of antiquity."[38] Could there be some truth to the map of "pre-sand Egypt," even if it was a copy of a copy of a copy? Did Gurdjieff possess a copy of a map dating back more than 5,000 years—perhaps even back to the end of the last Ice Age? Given that Gurdjieff mentions the Sphinx specifically, is this evidence that the Sphinx appeared on this map of "pre-sand Egypt," anticipating the work that John Anthony West and I carried out on the re-dating of the monument? Or was the story of the map just a convenient fiction on the part of Gurdjieff? Unless Gurdjieff's map is found, we may never know. Be that as it may, one thing I feel very confident about is that for more than 12,000 years—perhaps much longer—there have been (and still are) secret societies protecting and passing down secret knowledge.

Notes

1. See for instance: Philip Gardiner, *Secret Societies*, Franklin Lakes, New Jersey: New Page Books, 2007. I am familiar with claims that various secret societies and conspiracies trace their lineages back to Atlantis, universal serpent worship, Enoch, and similar notions; however, it is not possible in this short contribution to evaluate all of these various claims, many based on extremely circumstantial evidence, channeled insights, and the like. See for instance: W. Scott-Elliott, *The Story of Atlantis*, London: Theosophical Publishing Society, second and revised edition 1909, reprinted 1914. For a review of approaches to the issue of Atlantis, see: Joscelyn Godwin, *Atlantis and the Cycles of Time: Prophecies, Traditions, and Occult Revelations*, Rochester, Vermont: Inner Traditions, 2011. A note on dates: CE = Common Era; BCE = Before the Common Era.

2. John Anthony West, *Serpent in the Sky: The High Wisdom of Ancient Egypt* (revised edition), Wheaton, Illinois: Quest Books, 1993 [originally published by Harper and Row, 1979], p. 27. West's book is first and foremost a presentation and discussion of the Egyptological contributions of the Alsatian philosopher R.A. Schwaller de Lubicz.

3. West 1993, p. 24, italics in the original.

4. West 1993, p. 24.

5. West 1993, p. 25; British spelling of "civilisations" in the original.

6. Robert M. Schoch and Logan Yonavjak, compilers and commentators, *The Parapsychology Revolution: A Concise Anthology of*

Paranormal and Psychical Research, New York: Tarcher/Penguin, 2008.

7. West 1993 [note 2], p. 217.

8. See: West 1993, p. 217, and Jason Reza Jorjani, *Prometheus and Atlas*, unpublished doctoral dissertation, PhD in philosophy, The State University of New York–Stony Brook, 2014.

9. West 1993, p. 217.

10. West 1993, p. 217.

11. Robert M. Schoch, *Forgotten Civilization: The Role of Solar Outbursts in Our Past and Future*, Rochester, Vermont: Inner Traditions, 2012, pp. 99–100, 183–184.

12. Schoch 2012, pp. 249–252.

13. Schoch 2012, Chapter 2 ("The Great Sphinx").

14. I have visited Göbekli Tepe a number of times, often accompanied by my wife, Catherine (Katie) Ulissey, and thus much of my discussion of the site is based on my firsthand experiences. For an analysis of the fauna represented at Göbekli Tepe, see: Joris Peters and Klaus Schmidt, "Animals in the Symbolic World of Pre-Pottery Neolithic Göbekli Tepe, South-Eastern Turkey: A Preliminary Assessment," *Anthropozoologica*, Vol. 39, No. 1: 179–218 (2004). For a general discussion of Göbekli Tepe, see: Schoch 2012 [note 11], Chapter 3 ("Göbekli Tepe and the Origins of Civilization"). For a compilation of photographs of the site, and the standardized designations of the enclosures and pillars using various letters and numbers, see: Harry Eilenstein, *Göbekli Tepe: Die Bilderwelt des Tempels der Menschen*, Norderstedt: Books on Demand GmbH., 2011. (Note: The copyright is listed as 2009 but the copy I purchased in early 2013 was clearly updated since 2009, and includes photographs that my wife and I took during our trip to Göbekli Tepe in May 2010 and that Eilenstein somehow acquired and used in his book without our permission and without acknowledging us. On March 2,

2013, Amazon.com listed this book with a publication date of October 6, 2011.

15. Schoch 2012 [note 11], p. 54. Here it is important to review some of the most recent evidence pertaining to the dating of Göbekli Tepe. A radiocarbon date on crude secondary walls at Göbekli Tepe (constructed perhaps centuries after the original pillars were erected) of circa 9745 to 9314 BCE (Olivier Dietrich, 2013, *"PPND—the Platform for Neolithic Radiocarbon Dates: Göbekli Tepe,"* available at *www.exoriente.org/ associated_projects/ppnd_site.php?s=25*, accessed December 24, 2013) strongly suggests that the earliest and most sophisticated portions of the site date before the close of the Ice Age. This is in agreement with my analysis of an Orion alignment at circa 10,000 BCE for Enclosure D of the site (Schoch 2012 [note 11], pp. 53–57). Robert Bauval and Anu Nagappa concluded that the "Vulture Pillar" (Pillar 43) of Enclosure D indicates that the summer solstice was in the constellation Scorpio (Scorpius) when the structure was erected (R. Bauval, personal communication, November 7, 2013), which further corroborates a date of about 12,000 years ago for this portion of the site. Other portions of Göbekli Tepe may date to as much as 2,000 or more years later; thus the site spans the end of the last Ice Age. Alignments at Göbekli Tepe have also been suggested relative to Cygnus, circa 9400 BCE (Andrew Collins, 2013, "Göbekli Tepe: Its Cosmic Blueprint Revealed," available at *www.andrewcollins.com/page/articles/Gobekli .htm*, accessed December 24, 2013), and Sirius, circa 9100 BCE (Giulio Magli, 2013, "Sirius and the Project of the Megalithic Enclosures at Gobekli Tepe [sic]," available at *http://arxiv. org/ftp/arxiv/papers/1307/1307.8397.pdf*, accessed December 24, 2013). Based on my analyses, these are either secondary alignments or the researchers are simply mistaken.

16. As relayed by Graham Hancock in a posting on Facebook dated September 10, 2013.

17. Brian Hayden, "The Proof Is in the Pudding: Feasting and the Origins of Domestication," *Current Anthropology*, Vol. 50, No. 5 (October 2009), pp. 597–601; the reference to Göbekli Tepe appears on p. 599.

18. I have made the case elsewhere (Schoch 2012 [note 11]) that genuine civilization of a sophisticated nature existed prior to circa 9700 BCE, which was devastated by the events that brought the last Ice Age to a close—in my assessment, caused by major solar outbursts orders of magnitude more powerful than anything seen in the last few thousand years.

19. P. D. Ouspensky, *In Search of the Miraculous: Fragments of an Unknown Teaching*, New York: Harcourt, Brace, and Company, 1949.

20. Ouspensky 1949, pp. 31–32; italics in the original.

21. See: Robert M. Schoch, "What Lives On? Investigating Life After Death," *New Dawn* Special Issue 7, pp. 11–16 (2009); and Robert M. Schoch, "Easter Island and the Afterlife," *New Dawn*, January-February 2011, pp. 59–66.

22. John G. Bennett, *Talks on Beelzebub's Tales*, York Beach, Maine: Samuel Weiser, 1988, p. 25; material in brackets added by R. Schoch.

23. G.I. Gurdjieff, *Meetings With Remarkable Men*, New York: E. P. Dutton, 1969/1974, p. 87.

24. Gurdjieff 1969, p. 36; italics in the original; material in brackets added by R. Schoch.

25. Gurdjieff 1969, p. 37; material in brackets added by R. Schoch.

26. Gurdjieff 1969, p. 90.

27. Gurdjieff 1969, Chapter 7.

28. Michael Howard, *The Occult Conspiracy*, Rochester, Vermont: Destiny Books, 1989, pp. 27–28.

29. *Gobeklitepe: The World's First Temple*, directed by Ahmet Turgut Yazman, available on DVD from Maker Arts (Istanbul), 2011.

30. Klaus Schmidt, *Göbekli Tepe: A Stone Age Sanctuary in South-Eastern Anatolia.* Şanlıurfa, Turkey: ArchaeNova/ex oriente e.V. Berlin (special edition produced by ArchaeNova and printed in Turkey by Kurtuluş Matbaası, Şanlıurfa), 2012 (copy purchased on site at Göbekli Tepe, June 2013), p. 203.
31. Maker Arts 2011 [note 29].
32. Maker Arts 2011; for more information on Sidharth's research prior to his introduction to Göbekli Tepe, see: B.G. Sidharth, *The Celestial Key to the Vedas: Discovering the Origins of the World's Oldest Civilization*, Rochester, Vermont: Inner Traditions, 1999.
33. For an introduction to Dogon art, see such works as: Kate Ezra, *Art of the Dogon: Selections From the Lester Wunderman Collection*, New York: The Metropolitan Museum of Art (distributed by Harry N. Abrams, Inc.), 1988; Pascal James Imperato, *Dogon Cliff Dwellers: The Art of Mali's Mountain People*, New York: L. Kahan Gallery/African Arts, 1978; Pierre Langlois, *Art Soudanais: Tribus Dogon*, Brussels, Belgium: Editions de la Connaissance, 1954; Jean Laude, *African Art of the Dogon: The Myths of the Cliff Dwellers*, New York: The Brooklyn Museum in association with The Viking Press, 1973; F.H. Lem, *Sculptures Soudanaises*, Paris: Arts et Métiers Graphiques, 1948; see also, Robert M. Schoch, "Secrets of the Dogon: Does a Traditional African People Preserve Knowledge Inherited From Sophisticated Ancient Civilizations?" *Atlantis Rising*, #103 (January–February 2014), pp. 40, 67–68.
34. Sculpture currently in a private American collection; for a related example showing a similar H formed by two figures on either side of the navel, see: Hélène Leloup, *Dogon*, Paris: Musée de Quai Branly & Somogy Editions D'Art, 2011, pp. 348–349. (This sculpture is also illustrated on the front cover of the dust jacket of the hardcover edition.)
35. May 19, 2013 presentation at Megalithomania in Glastonbury, UK.

36. See also the discussion of Mount Du-Ku in Schmidt 2012 [note 30], p. 207.
37. Gurdjieff 1969 [note 23], p. 99.
38. Gurdjieff 1969, p. 120.

Monsters of the Stones

By Nick Redfern

Cryptozoology is the study of unknown animals. Science, particularly mainstream zoology, denies that these animals exist at all. Such animals include lake monsters, sea serpents, the chupacabras, and the Jersey Devil. There is a sub-section of cryptozoology that concerns itself with the study of so-called man-beasts. It's a realm in which Bigfoot, hairy wild men, Mothman, the Abominable Snowman, and werewolves lurk. Although most cryptozoologists take the view that these humanoid horrors are nothing more than flesh-and-blood creatures of presently unidentified types, the evidence strongly suggests otherwise.

There are, for example, numerous reports on file in which eyewitnesses have encountered monstrous man-beasts in the vicinity of (a) ancient stone circles, (b) burial mounds that date back thousands of years, and (c) sites of profound archaeological significance. This has given rise to an intriguing theory, namely, that these "creatures" are actually nothing of the sort; rather, they are supernatural guardians created by powerful shamanic figures in times long gone to protect sacred locales where the ancients dutifully worshipped. Today, thousands of years after they were first unleashed, those same hideous creations are still faithfully patrolling and guarding the landscape, very much as they did millennia ago.

From Skinwalkers to Tulpas

Linda Godfrey is one of the world's leading authorities on the phenomenon of werewolves, and the author of such fine pieces of essential reading as *The Michigan Dogman* and *The Beast of Bray Road*. Of the much-feared Native American phenomenon known as the skinwalker—an entity created via supernatural rituals that resembles an animal but is essentially a spirit-based doppelganger of a shaman—Godfrey notes that they watch over sacred sites and are linked to the controversial phenomenon of the tulpa. It was actually a woman named Alexandra David-Neel who brought the idea of the tulpa to the Western world, all the way from the Himalayas. David-Neel (born Louise Eugenie Alexandrine Marie David in France in October 1868) was the first woman to gain the title of a Tibetan lama. A committed Buddhist who lived to the highly impressive age of 100, she was a noted traveler who had a deep passion and love for Asia, particularly the Himalayas—home, interestingly enough, to the famous Abominable Snowman, or Yeti.

Essentially, a tulpa is an enigmatic life form that has its origins within the mysterious depths of the human mind. When carefully focused upon by the creator, dutifully nurtured, and significantly empowered over an extensive period of time, however, the tulpa can break free of its moorings in the mind and take on a degree of independent reality. In simple terms, what we imagine *internally*, when we quite literally put our minds to it, can manifest into full-blown reality of an *external* nature—that is, into matter.

Walter Yeeling Evans-Wentz, a writer, anthropologist, and pioneer in the study of Tibetan Buddhism, said of the tulpa concept: "Inasmuch as the mind creates the world of appearances, it can create any particular object desired. The process consists of giving palpable being to a visualization, in very much the same manner as an architect gives concrete expression in three dimensions to his abstract concepts after first having given them expression in the two-dimensions of his blue-print" (Evans-Wentz, 2000).

Is it truly feasible that enigmas such as Bigfoot and its ilk are not merely biological anomalies, but something born of the human mind and given a specific task to perform—namely, to guard the revered landscapes of our ancestors? As controversial as it may sound, when we go looking for evidence in support of such a theory, we actually find it. And no place is more representative of this than the British Isles.

A BRONZE AGE WARRIOR

R.C.C. Clay, a noted historian, had an encounter with one of these mysterious entities while driving past Bottlebush Down, Dorset, England—an area peppered with ancient sites—during the final days of 1924. The story, however, did not surface until the mid-1950s, when Clay shared the details with an authority on all things ghostly and spectral, James Wentworth Day, who penned such titles as *Here Are Ghosts and Witches*, *A Ghost Hunter's Game Book*, *In Search of Ghosts*, and *They Walk the Wild Places*. The location of the nightmarish encounter that Clay related to Day was the A3081 road, which is situated between the Dorset villages of Cranborne and Sixpenny Handley, on farmland known locally as Bottlebush Down. It was while Clay was driving home after spending a day excavating in the area, and as the daylight was giving way to dusk, that he encountered something extraordinary. Maybe even *beyond* extraordinary.

At a point where the new road crossed with an old Roman road, a cloaked horseman, riding wildly and at high speed on the back of a huge and muscular stallion, seemingly appeared out of nowhere. But there was something wrong about this man, something *terribly* wrong. It is fortunate that the witness in this case was Clay—a man with an expert and profound knowledge of English history, folklore, and times and people long gone. Having kept the rider in careful sight for about 300 feet, there was no doubt in Clay's mind that the rider's clothing and weapon firmly identified him as nothing less than a denizen of the Bronze Age—which, incredibly, would have placed his origins somewhere between 2100 and 750 BC. Not surprisingly, with darkness falling fast, Clay floored the accelerator and headed for home, somewhat shakily but decidedly excited, too.

And there is one other thing that should be kept in mind. In fact, it's arguably the most important aspect of the entire story. Of all the people that the ancient horseman should have appeared for, it was a man, R.C.C. Clay, who had spent the very day in question excavating—or, rather, *disturbing*—a Bronze Age earthworks, something that may have understandably enraged any self-respecting tulpa guardian.

WHEN PAST AND PRESENT CROSS

W.E. Thorner was stationed on the island of Hoy, off the north coast of Scotland, during the Second World War when he saw a group of wild men dancing on the top of a cliff at Thorness—rather notably, a sacred and magical place named after the Norse god of the dwarfs—at the height of a tumultuous winter thunderstorm. In Thorner's own, captivating words:

> These creatures were small in stature, but they did not have long noses nor did they appear kindly in demeanor. They possessed round faces, sallow in complexion, with long, dark, bedraggled hair. As they danced about, seeming to throw themselves over the cliff edge, I felt that I was a witness to some ritual dance of a tribe of primitive men. It is difficult to describe in a few words my feelings at this juncture or my bewilderment. The whole sequence could have lasted about three minutes until I was able to leave the cliff edge (Marwick, 1975).

Similar to Thorne's account is the story of a noted Devon, England folklorist and acclaimed writer named Theo Brown. The author of such titles as *Devon Ghosts* and *Family Holidays Around Dartmoor*, Brown told the story of a friend of hers who had been walking alone at dusk near the Neolithic earthworks at the top of Lustleigh Cleave, which sits on the extreme east side of Dartmoor, in the Wrey Valley. Lustleigh Cleave is an extraordinarily strange place at the best of times, one where an inordinate number of unexplained incidents seem to take place on an amazingly regular basis. Moreover, the remains of prehistoric stone huts can be seen in the direct vicinity, and an ancient burial monument, Datuidoc's Stone—which is estimated to have originated at some point around 550 to 600 AD—still stands to this very day, pretty much as it did all those thousands of years ago.

Jonathan Downes, director of the British-based Center for Fortean Zoology, says of the weirdness that dominates Lustleigh Cleave: "I have got reports of sightings of a ghostly Tudor hunting party, of mysterious lights in the sky, and even the apparitions of a pair of Roman Centurions at Lustleigh Cleave." But, adds Downes, getting to the most important aspect of the story, "Theo Brown's friend saw, clearly, a family of 'cave men,' either naked and covered in hair or wrapped in the shaggy pelts of some wild animal, shambling around the stone circle at the top of the cleave" (Downes, 2004).

Conjuring up a Neanderthal

The late Stan Gooch, the author of a number of books, including *Creatures From Inner Space*, told of his encounter with what appeared to be nothing less than a Neanderthal man at a séance held at a house in the English city of Coventry in the 1950s. In Gooch's very own words, during the course of the séance, something both primitive and primeval materialized before the shocked attendees:

> This was a crouching ape-like shape, which became clearer as the moments passed. I guess it approximated to most people's idea of what an ancient cave man would look like. Yet one could not make out too much detail—the eyes were hidden, for example. It stood in half shadow, watching us, breathing heavily as if nervous. I must say, though, that I sensed rather

than heard the breathing. I could not decide whether our visitor was wearing the skin of some animal, or whether it had a rough coat of hair of its own" (Gooch, 1978).

All attempts to question the man-beast and have it join the circle were utterly fruitless, and eventually it melted away into nothingness. Nevertheless, Gooch never forgot the experience and later mused upon the notion that what he had seen on that fateful evening was a "classic Neanderthal." Rather interestingly, Gooch penned a number of books in later years, including *The Neanderthal Question* and *The Neanderthal Legacy*, which theorized that we, as *Homo sapiens*, are the result of a hybrid mix of Cromagnon man and Neanderthal man (Ibid.).

The Rollright Stones in 1919. Image from Wikimedia Commons.

Gooch was of the opinion that what he conjured up was the spirit of a long-dead primitive human. That Gooch admitted to being obsessed by the nature, lives, and legacies of the Neanderthals *prior* to his encounter, however, suggests he may very well have inadvertently created a tulpa-like Neanderthal, rather than having literally raised the dead—and perhaps in a fashion not unlike that of the magicians of yesteryear.

The Stones of the Witch

Now we come to the Rollright Stones, which are situated near Long Compton, a centuries-old little village in the English county of Oxfordshire. Collectively, they are comprised of a tomb, known as the Whispering Knights, a classic circle of stones called the King's Men, and a solitary stone referred to as the King's Stone. As for the time of the construction of the Rollright Stones, this appears to be a clear-cut issue: the Neolithic and Bronze Age eras.

As with Stonehenge, legends and pet theories abound as to the particular origin of the Stones. Certainly, the most engaging is that which surfaced in 1610 from a historian named William Camden. The story goes that the stones were not always stones. They were originally an unnamed visiting king and his faithful knights who were turned to stone—in classic Gorgon-style, one might well suggest—by a legendary local witch, one Mother Shipton. The king, not surprisingly, became the King's Stone, and the bulk of his men were turned into the King's Men. The few who had initially avoided—but not for long, unfortunately—Mother Shipton's malevolent powers collectively became the Whispering Knights.

In 1977, author Paul Devereux established what became known as the Dragon Project, the purpose of which was to study claims that certain British prehistoric sites had unusual forces or energies attached to them, including magnetic, infrared, and ultrasonic anomalies. While investigating none other than the Rollright Stones, Devereux reported that one of the team members—a well-known archaeologist—was sitting in a van when an unidentified, hair-covered beast of considerable size walked by. An instant later it utterly vanished, never to reappear.

The Creature of the Nine Ladies

Jonathan Downes reminisces on another case of relevance:

One of the most credible reports brought to my attention came from a family that had a daylight encounter with a large and hairy beast in the Peak District [England] in 1991. This all occurred as they were driving near Ladybower Reservoir on the Manchester to Sheffield road. On a hillside, one of the family members had spotted a large figure walking down towards the road. But this was no man.

They brought the car to a screeching halt and came face to face with an enormous creature about eight feet tall, that was covered in long, brown hair with eyes just like a man's. Its walk was different, too, almost crouching. But just as the man-beast reached the road, another car pulled up behind the family and blasted their horn—apparently wondering why they had stopped in the middle of the road. Suddenly, the creature—which I presume was startled by the noise—ran across the road, jumped over a wall that had a 10-foot drop on the other side, and ran off, disappearing into the woods. Now, I know that the family has returned to the area but has seen nothing since (Redfern, 2012).

The case to which Jon refers was also studied deeply by paranormal investigator Martin Jeffrey, who was able to speak in person with the family in question and determined that the incident occurred on a Sunday afternoon in November 1991. The family told Jeffrey: "We don't think he's dangerous...just a creature left behind by evolution" (Jeffrey, 1998).

It's also worth noting that, with regard to the sighting of the large and lumbering beast near the Peak District–based Ladybower Reservoir in November 1991, less than one mile away, on Stanton Moor stands a stone circle called the Nine Ladies. It was constructed during the Bronze Age era, and is a place where modern-day druids and pagans celebrate the summer solstice every year. As the legend goes, the circle takes its name from nine women who were turned to stone as punishment for dancing on Sundays.

Perhaps, in light of this extraordinary evidence, when it comes to such cases we should be focusing our attention far *less* on what's going on in the relevant location of ancient stone circles right now,

Stonehenge as it looks today. Photograph by the author.

and far *more* on (a) the matter of what may have occurred there centuries or millennia ago, and (b) the issue of what—in some strange, ethereal, and wild form—may continue to linger and wander and, sometimes, terrorize the good folk of Britain.

The Stonehenge Man-Beast

Merrily Harpur, the author of the book *Mystery Big Cats*, has logged a fascinating account from one George Price, who had an undeniably bizarre experience on Salisbury Plain in September 2002, while then serving with the British Army. It was at the height of a military exercise, Harpur was told, and Price was a "commander in the turret of our tank, and we were advancing to contact our warriors." Suddenly, Price's attention was drawn to a "large, ape-like figure" that "looked scared because of the noise from the engines and tanks were moving at speed all around" (Harpur, 2011). Although the beast was not in sight for long—it raced for the safety of "nearby prickly shrubs"—an amazed Price could see that "its fur was similar to an orangutan's in color...its height was impressive...[and] it seemed to run with its back low, i.e. bent over" (Ibid.).

Salisbury Plain is not just home to military maneuvers, however. It is also home to one of the world's most famous ancient stone circles: Stonehenge. While most students of the legendary structure conclude it had its beginnings somewhere around 3100 BC, evidence of human activity and even ritualistic activities in the area has been found suggesting a presence as far back as 8000 BC. But regardless of when, precisely, large-scale construction of Stonehenge actually began, what can be said with certainty is that it is comprised of a ditch, a bank, and what are known as the Aubrey holes—round pits in the chalk that form a huge circle. And then, of course, there are those massive stone blocks.

No fewer than 82 of Stonehenge's so-called bluestones, some of which weigh up to four tons, are believed to have been transported from the Preseli Mountains in southwest Wales to the Wiltshire site, a distance of approximately 240 miles. However, the actual number of stones is in dispute because barely more than 40 remain today. Certainly, such a herculean operation to move such huge stones would be no easy feat in the modern era, never mind thousands of years ago. And yet, somehow, this incredible and mystifying task was successfully achieved.

Stonehenge's 30 giant Sarsen stones, meanwhile, were brought from the Marlborough Downs, a distance of around 25 miles from

Castle Ring today. Photograph by the author.

the site. Although this might sound like a much easier task than having to haul the bluestones all the way from Wales, this is hardly the case: As noted, the Welsh stones are in the order of four tons each; however, some of the Sarsen stones from the downs weigh in at 25 tons, the heaviest at around 50. And people wonder why so much mystery and intrigue surrounds the creation of Stonehenge?

Is it possible that what George Price saw on Salisbury Plain was not actually a British Bigfoot, but perhaps something akin to R.C.C. Clay's Bronze Age warrior, but one with a long-gone link to the nearby Stonehenge?

AN ENCOUNTER AT CASTLE RING

Reports of hairy wild men abound throughout the English county of Staffordshire, but there is one area of the county that seems to attract a great deal more than its fair share of such activity. Its name is hauntingly familiar to one and all throughout the area as Castle Ring. Located near the village of Cannock Wood, Castle Ring is an Iron Age structure commonly known as a Hill Fort. It is 801 feet above sea level, and its main ditch and bank enclosure is 14 feet high and, at its widest point, 853 feet across.

Admittedly very little is known about the mysterious and long-forgotten people who built Castle Ring, except to say that they were already in residence at the time of the Roman invasion of AD 43 and remained there until approximately AD 50. Some suggest that the initial foundations of Castle Ring may even have been laid as early as 500 BC. Moreover, historians suggest that the creators of Castle Ring might have represented a powerful body of people that held firm sway over certain other parts of Staffordshire, as well as significant portions of both Shropshire and Cheshire at the time in question. While the enigmatic creators of Castle Ring exited our world millennia ago, and left us with very little solid knowledge of who they were or what they actually represented, Castle Ring can claim to play host to far stranger entities, including monstrous beasts.

On May 1, 2004, Alec Williams was driving past the car park that sits at the base of Castle Ring when he witnessed a hair-covered, manlike entity lumber across the road and into the trees. A shocked Williams stated that the sighting lasted barely a few seconds, but that he was able to make out its amazing form: "It was about seven feet tall, with short, shiny, dark brown hair, a large head and had eyes that glowed bright red." Interestingly, Williams stated that as he slowed his vehicle down, he witnessed something akin to a camera flash coming from the depths of the woods and heard a strange, hooting cry that sounded like "Hoo!" (Redfern, 2004).

Neolithic Nightmares

In 2012, I conducted an extensive interview with one of England's most respected seekers of strange creatures, Neil Arnold.

Nick Redfern and Neil Arnold. Photograph by the author.

When it comes to the matter of what might be termed "created creatures," Arnold's comments and observations are noteworthy, to say the least. He told me:

> I've always wondered what type of manifestation these U.K. wild men could be. In the autumn of 2011 a psychic lady whom I know as a friend and whom I trust accompanied me to Blue Bell Hill, which is a very haunted village in Kent, a few miles short of the town of Maidstone. I knew of several obscure man-beast reports in the area, which she knew nothing about. I took her to one particular spot near some ancient stones, hoping she'd pick up a ghostly presence, and she said

she felt nothing whatsoever. But she did state quite categorically that a few years previous, around 2003, she'd had a bizarre encounter in the area one night (Redfern, 2012).

The stones in question are collectively known as Kit's Coty House, a set of Neolithic stones said to be older than Stonehenge, and which jut from a field at Blue Bell Hill. These stones have a lot of folklore attached to them. Some suggest they are used as a calendar, or could mark where a great and bloody battle once took place. Others believe the stones were once used for sacrificial purposes, and there are those who opt for the more fanciful rumor that they were constructed by witches on the proverbial dark and stormy night.

A HOUSE OF HORRORS

The story told to Arnold goes like this: "She had visited Kit's Coty House with a group of fellow psychics. Her friends were over on one side of the field which harbors the stones and she was in another area when she noticed someone walking towards her a few hundred yards away. The figure seemed to be striding rather aggressively and was coming from the direction of a thicket which runs alongside the field" (Redfern, 2012). This was no normal human of modern-day standards, however, as Arnold's next words make acutely and abundantly clear:

> The woman, whose name is Corriene, stated that from a distance the figure appeared huge in build and covered in hair and she sensed it was not real but gave off an air of malevolence. The figure marched towards her and she could see it had long hair and a beard, covering most of its face. The hulking figure was taller than six feet and appeared to have a loincloth around its waist and furred boots. No-one else saw this figure, but I was intrigued as I knew that in the past several witnesses had come forward to say they'd seen similar figures in woods within miles of Blue Bell Hill (Ibid.).

It was this encounter that set Arnold on a decidedly intriguing train of thought:

I began to wonder if people had seen, from a distance, some type of ghostly primitive man—long hair, bearded, muscular, animal fur around the waist—who, from several hundred yards away, or in ill light, may have looked as if he was covered in hair. Blue Bell Hill and much of Kent is steeped in history, so maybe people were seeing some type of Neolithic hunter. Corriene was intrigued by what I said and then, rather startled, mentioned that on another occasion whilst in the area of the stones she'd seen several of these people whom she felt were not aggressive, and although armed with spears were simply guarding the area and stooping low in the bushes, curious as to what they were seeing (Ibid.).

Significantly, this case was not an aberration, as Arnold told me:

In 1974 a woman named Maureen—whom I became very close friends with after working with her 10 years ago—was with her boyfriend in the woods off a close named Sherwood Avenue, in Walderslade, which, as the crow flies, is only a couple of miles [from] Blue Bell Hill. Her boyfriend was tending to the fire when Maureen felt as if she was being watched. She turned slowly and to her amazement saw a massive figure, standing over seven feet tall, seemingly covered in hair, just a few yards away. The figure had bright eyes which blinked. The figure seemed to crouch down behind the bushes very slowly, and Maureen asked her boyfriend if they could leave the area, [which] they did. Maureen never told her boyfriend what she'd seen. They eventually married and were together for many years. In fact, she never told anyone about what she'd seen until she realized what I was interested in (Ibid.).

A 2011 DEVELOPMENT

It's important to note here that Neil Arnold is inclined to give a high degree of credence to the tulpa theory. In January 2012 Arnold told me that on the night of August 24 of the previous year (2011) he was taking two women and their boyfriends on a private tour of Blue Bell Hill when amazing and unsettling events occurred:

It was about 9:30 at night—pitch black—when we passed the [Kit's Coty House] stones and headed down into a dark corner of woodland. I was about to tell them about the man-beast sighting and had my back to the woods when they all screamed in tandem. It was funny seeing two grown men turn white as a ghost. They all stated that about twenty yards behind me in the woods, a tall, dark, muscular figure had run through the woods and vanished. I never saw this because as I said, my back was to the woods. They all frantically shone torches, but there was nothing.

I do have a belief that some of these entities exist due to thought and be made unintentionally stronger when given attention, whether it's through newspaper reports, people talking about the creature, etc. I do not believe these things occur in the physical sense. I believe they exist on an astral level and are triggered. I believe the human mind and culture manifests these things and sometimes, if we believe in them enough, they are given strength (Ibid.).

~~~

As we have seen time and again, in those sacred, ancient sites where modern-day humanity intrudes, there is very often a sudden triggering of an equally ancient creature that is perceived as threatening or frightening, and that succeeds in driving us away. Based upon all of the evidence recounted previously, it is likely these paranormal, tulpa-type entities will continue to faithfully patrol those millennia-old places of paranormal power for as long as we blunder and bluster our way around them.

BIBLIOGRAPHY

"The Ancients of Lustleigh Cleave." *www.legendarydartmoor.co.uk/ancients_cleave.htm*. November 22, 2007.

Arnold, Neil. *The Mystery Animals of the British Isles: Kent.* Woolsery, UK: CFZ Press, 2009.

"Bottlebush Down." *www.ghosts.org.uk/ghost/3255/haunted/road/bottlebush-down/cranborne.html*. 2012.

"Castle Ring (Staffordshire)." *www.megalithic.co.uk/article php?sid=4982*. 2012.

Chippindale, Christopher. *Stonehenge Complete.* London: Thames & Hudson, 2004.

David-Neel, Alexandra. *Magic and Mystery in Tibet.* New York: Dover Publications, Inc., 1971.

Downes, Jonathan. *Monster Hunter.* Woolsery, UK: CFZ Press, 2004.

Evans-Wentz, W.Y. *The Tibetan Book of the Great Liberation.* New York: Oxford University Press, 2000.

Godfrey, Linda S. *Real Wolfmen.* New York: Tarcher, 2012.

Gooch, Stan. *The Para-Normal.* New York: Harper & Row, 1978.

"Guide to the W. Y. (Walter Yeeling) Evans-Wentz Papers, 1894-1961": *www.oac.cdlib.org/findaid ark:/13030tf900006xp/*. 2009.

Harpur, Merrily. "The ABC X-Files," *Fortean Times*, No. 278, October 2011.

Jeffrey, Martin. "The Big Hairy Encounter." *Mystery Magazine. http://homepage.ntlworld.com/chris.mullins/DERBYSHIRE%20 BHM.htm*. February 1998.

Lambrick, George. *The Rollright Stones*. London: English Heritage, 1988.

Marwick, Ernest. *The Folklore of Orkney and Shetland*. Lanham, Md.: Rowman & Littlefield, 1975.

Newall, R.S. *Stonehenge, Wiltshire—Ancient Monuments and Historic Buildings*. London: Her Majesty's Stationery Office, 1959.

"Nine Ladies Stone Circle." *www.english-heritage.org.uk/daysout/ properties/nine-ladies-stone-circle/*. 2013.

"Paul Devereux Speaking at the Rollright Stones: Part 1, The Dragon Project." *www.megalithic.co.uk/mm/book/devereux1trans.htm*. 2011.

Redfern, Nick. Interview with Alec Williams, June 22, 2004.

———. Interview with Jonathan Downes, May 16, 2012.

———. Interview with Neil Arnold, January 14, 2012.

———. "The Horror of the Horseman." *http://mysteriousuniverse. org/2013/10/the-horror-of-the-horseman/*. October 31, 2012.

"The Rollright Stones." *www.rollrightstones.co.uk/index.php/stones/*. 2011.

"The Salisbury Plain Training Area." *www.eng-h.gov.uk/archrev/ rev95_6/salisbry.htm*. 2011.

PLATO'S ATLANTIS: FACT OR FICTION?

BY FRANK JOSEPH

To a majority of Americans and virtually every mainstream scientist, Atlantis was only a myth. Even scholars more open to factual possibilities for the lost city are far from agreement concerning its origins, age, location, size, manner of destruction, or significance. They see Atlantis in the Canary Islands, the Azores, the Bahamas, Cuba, Spain, Malta, Scotland, Sweden, Germany, North America, Mexico, Crete, Cyprus, Bolivia, and even the Pacific Ocean. According to such scholars, Atlantis was, variously, as huge as a continent—Antarctica or the whole of South America—or no larger than just part Santorini, a tiny island in the eastern Mediterranean Sea. It was the first civilization, technologically modern and beyond, an Ice Age tribal society, a Bronze Age empire, a Minoan outpost, or a Greek Classical period town destroyed by a volcano, tsunami, earthquake, pole shift, comet, asteroid, flying saucer attack, or social suicide anywhere from more than 100,000 years ago to as recently as 430 BC.

These wildly contrary theories and conclusions have muddled the debate for too long, but they may be largely reconciled by close scrutiny of the most complete source material still extant after more than two millennia. Strangely, for all the thousands of books, magazine articles, television documentaries, and feature films about Atlantis, its oldest surviving account, although generally acknowledged by opponents on either side, is rarely, if ever consulted in detail. They routinely and proudly cite its renowned author to lend their own versions

59

special credence, but mostly ignore the guidance spelled out so precisely in his dialogues, the *Timaeus* and *Kritias*.

Indeed, a more credible advocate of Atlantis-as-fact is more impossible to imagine than Plato, "founder of the Academy in Athens, the first institution of higher learning in the Western world," who "helped to lay the foundations of Western philosophy and science."[1] English mathematician Alfred North Whitehead, himself described as the "greatest speculative mind of [the 20th] century," stated that "the safest general characterization of the European philosophical tradition is that it consists of a series of footnotes to Plato."[2] Yet, skeptics claim that Plato merely invented Atlantis to dramatize the ideal state. They fail to realize, however, that he had already delineated his envisioned society in *The Republic*, the opposite of Atlantean imperialism.

On the contrary, he depicted Atlantis as a corrupt culture meriting destruction. In this he did not once only and uncharacteristically turn away from philosophy to history, but used Atlantis as an historical parallel to illustrate his philosophical point; namely, the degenerate causes leading to an originally virtuous society's downfall. To empower his argument, the illustration he chose must, of necessity, have been a real place, suffering an actual fate with which his listeners were already familiar. For example, in 430 BC, when Plato was about two years old, "a major earthquake caused widespread destruction and tsunami inundation around the Gulf of Evvia," in Euboea, southeastern Greece.[3] An off-shore island partially collapsed into the sea and was subsequently renamed *Atalanti*, together with its equally devastated vicinity, after Atlantis, whose fate it mirrored.

Earlier still, women participants at the annual Panathenea festival in Athens wore a *peplum*, a broad skirt embroidered with scenes depicting Athena's victory over the forces of Atlantis—not a particularly remarkable fact in itself, except that the Panathenea was celebrated 125 years prior to Plato's birth. About the same time, the historian Hellanicus of Lesbos authored a manuscript entitled *Atlantis*, only fragments of which survive in the *Oxyrhynchus Papyri*, so named after the ancient a city of Oxyrhynchus, today's el-Bahnasa, where it was discovered during 1882, in Upper Egypt, approximately 100 miles south-southwest of Cairo. What little of the text remains indicates Hellanicus was not concerned with Atalanti's contemporaneous earthquake, tsunami, and incomplete submersion, which nevertheless may have inspired him to write about the much older, reminiscent, if far more catastrophic event. More famously, Herodotus discussed the Atlanteans in his *History* some 20 years before Plato was born.

It is clear then that Plato's fellow Greeks were at least fundamentally aware of the sunken city he showcased to make his point about the rise and fall of civilization. So, too, his account was verified after he died in 347 BC. Eight centuries later, the last major Greek philosopher cited the veracity of Plato's Atlantis account in *Platonis theologiam* ("Platonic theology"). Proclus pointed out that Egyptian columns inscribed with the story, as described in the *Kritias*, were visited and identically translated more than half a century after Plato's death.[4] They were personally examined by yet another influential thinker, Krantor of Soluntum, an *amicus Plato, sed magis amicus veritas*: "Plato's friend and a powerful friend of truth," according to Proclus.[5] Krantor had traveled to the Egyptian city of Sais, as part of his research for Plato's first biography, near the end of the fourth century BC, about 35 years after Plato died. Proclus reported that Krantor found the Atlantis report preserved there exactly as described in the *Timaeus* and *Kritias*.[6]

In 1956, Albert Rivand, professor of classical history at the Sorbonne, declared that both dialogues embodied ancient, historic traditions and contained results of the latest contemporary research carried out in Plato's day.[7] As translator Ivan Lissner observed, "That a distinguished French scholar who had spent decades studying the Platonic texts should reach this conclusion is most significant, because it invests the geographical and ontological allusions in the two books with greater weight."[8] R. Catesby Taliaferro writes in the foreword to the authoritative Thomas Taylor translation of *The Timaeus and the Kritias*:

It appears to me to be at least as well attested as any other narration in any ancient historian. Indeed, he [Plato] who proclaims that "truth is the source of every good both to gods and men," and the whole of whose works consists in detecting error and exploring certainty, can never be supposed to have willfully deceived mankind by publishing an extravagant romance as matter of fact, with all the precision of historical narrative. [9]

Plato, moreover, repeatedly insists throughout his Atlantis account on its veracity: "it is not fiction, but true history," "the wisest of the seven wise men once vouched its truth," "we may safely retain all that has been truthfully said," and so on.[10] Given their convincing verisimilitude and profusion of information they provide, the dialogues answer every fundamental question about the lost civilization, if only we closely examine all their details. Plato tells us that the story had been inscribed in Egyptian hieroglyphs on pillars inside a large temple. The structure, nothing of which remains today, was situated "at the head of the Delta, where the Nile divides, a district called the Saitic," outside the ancient city of Sau, present-day Sa-el-Hager, known to the Greeks as Sais, dedicated to the goddess Neith.[11]

As the divine patroness of wisdom, she provided a proper setting for ancient record-keeping. It was her temple that Solon, the great legislator and founder of Athenian democracy, visited around 590 BC. A high priest translated the account, which Solon took back with him to Greece. It passed down about 230 years later to Plato, who included its highlights in a pair of dialogues. The earlier was named after Timaeus of Locri, a Greek Pythagorean philosopher from Italy, author of a lost work *On the Soul of the Universe*. The other derived from Kritias, author of similarly lost tragedies and first cousin of Plato's mother. Because the territory of Atlantis is said to have been "larger than Libya and Asia combined," some investigators have jumped to the conclusion that it was a continent.[12]

Aside from the scientific facts that the sea floor of the North Atlantic Ocean is too weak to have ever supported a continental landmass, and that nothing of the kind has been found there by geologists, the Libya and Asia of Solon's or Plato's day in no way matched those regions as they are presently known. During the Classical Era, "Libya" was a thin strip of habitation sites running westward along the Mediterranean coast, perhaps 200 miles across North Africa from the Egyptian frontier. "Asia" signified only the western coast of Turkey, which included various kingdoms from the Dardanelles, entrance to the Black Sea in the north, southward to Mediterranean shores. Together, these regions could not comprise a "continent." Indeed, Plato used the term *nesos*, or "island," in referring to the Atlantean homeland.[13]

He was no less specific in describing its location, which was "opposite the strait you call the Pillars of Heracles," or Strait of Gibraltar, with "the furthest part of the island towards the Pillars of Heracles, and facing the district now called Gadeiros," today's Cadiz, in the south of Spain.[14] In other words, he tells us that a large island lay amid the waters between Morocco in the south and Portugal-Spain in the north, its eastern extremity pointing at Gibraltar on a parallel as far as Cadiz.

The *Kritias* explains how the island of Atlantis was blessed with "a plentiful variety of woodland to supply abundant timber for every kind of manufacture," recalling relatively nearby Madeira, which derived its name, "wood," from the island's dense forests.[15] Atlantis was also a typical Atlantic Ocean isle favored with uncommonly rich soil, just as the Canaries and Azores are notable for their volcanic fertility. The incongruous appearance of elephants in Plato's account was used by skeptics to fault it until 1967, when literally hundreds of pachyderm bones from some 40 different locations were unexpectedly dredged up by oceanographers excavating the ocean floor about 200 miles off the Portuguese coast.[16]

"The region as a whole was said to be high above the level of the sea, from which it arose precipitously," and featured mountains "more numerous, higher and more beautiful than any which exist today. And in them were numerous villages and a wealthy population, as well as rivers and lakes and meadows, which provided ample pasture for all kinds of domesticated and wild animals." The mountains surrounded "a uniformly flat plain ... rectangular in shape, measuring 341 miles in length and, at its mid-point, 228 miles in breadth from the coast. This whole area of the island faced south, and was sheltered from the north winds." Here, Plato informs us that the Atlantean island's roughly oblong or "rectangular" dimensions averaged—taking into consideration areas on the opposite flanks of the mountains, "which came right down to the sea"—350 miles long from east to west, and 233 miles north to south.[17]

Reaching into the Atlantic Ocean from its easternmost limits in the Gulf of Cadiz, the island's westernmost extent would have coincided with the Horseshoe Seamounts, a collection of underwater mountains which formerly stood above sea level as islands. Notable among them is the Ampere Seamount, known to have been dry land as recently as 8,000 years ago, if not much later, and the focus of Soviet oceanographers from the early 1970s to the mid-1980s, when they claimed to have observed grand staircases, building foundations, and stone walls on the slopes of sunken Mount Ampere.[18]

Returning to the great Atlantean plain, it "was naturally a long, regular rectangle," encompassed by an irrigation canal 100 feet deep, 600 feet wide, and 1,137 miles long, since it was dug out right around the plain.

The rivers that flowed down from the mountains emptied into it, and it made a complete circuit of the plain, running round from the city [of Atlantis, that stood at the center of the plain] from both directions, and there discharging into the sea. Channels about 100 feet broad were cut from the ditch's landward limb straight across the plain and a distance of 11 miles from each other, until they ran into it on its seaward side. [The Atlantean irrigation engineers] cut cross-channels between them and also to the city, and used the whole complex to float timber down from the mountains and transport seasonal abundance by boat. They had two harvests a year, a winter one for which they relied on rainfall, and a summer one for which the channels, fed by the rivers, provided irrigation.[19]

The first glimpse of Atlantis visitors had arriving by ship on the island's south coast would have been "a wall beginning at the sea, and running right round in a circle at the uniform distance of more than five-and-a-half miles from the largest [of three harbors] and returning on itself at the mouth of a canal to the sea." This canal was

300 feet wide, 100 feet deep, and nearly six miles long from the sea to the outermost ring [of the city of Atlantis], thus making it accessible from the sea, like a harbor. And [the Atlantean construction engineers] made the entrance to it large enough to admit the largest ships.... The wall was densely built up all around with houses. The canal and large harbor were crowded with vast numbers of merchant ships from all quarters, from which arose a constant din of shouting and noise, day and night.[20]

Behind the great wall lay the city of Atlantis. Its name means, literally, "the daughter of Atlas," the titan depicted in Classical myth as a naked, bearded man hefting the sphere of the heavens or zodiac on his shoulders, because he was the founder of astronomy and astrology. Atlas was often envisioned as a mountain with its summit shrouded in clouds, as though supporting the sky. The pre-Greek root of his name is *atla*, Sanskrit for "the upholder." "Atlantis" implies that the city was the creation of its first king, Atlas. From a

bird's-eye view, it would have resembled an immense target of con-
centric circles, comprising

> two rings of land and three of sea, like cartwheels, with an
> island at their center, and equidistant from each other. In each
> of these ring-islands they built many temples for different
> gods, and many gardens and areas for exercise, some for men,
> and some for horses.... At the bridges [which spanned the trio
> of great moats to connect with the central island] they made
> channels through the rings of land which separated those of
> water, large enough to admit the passage of a single trireme [a
> large battleship with three banks of oars], and roofed over to
> make an underground tunnel, for the rims of the rings were
> of some height above sea-level...the rings and the bridges,
> which were 100 feet broad, were enclosed by a stone wall all
> around, with towers and gates guarding the bridges on either
> side where they cross the water. The stone for them, which
> was red, white and black [respectively, tufa, pumice and lava,
> characteristic of a volcanic environment, like that of neigh-
> boring Madeira, the Canary and Azore islands], they cut out
> from the central island and the outer and inner rings of land,
> and, in the process, excavated pairs of hollow docks with
> roofs of rock. Some of their buildings were of a single color;
> in others, they mixed different colored stone.

> The largest of the rings, to which there was access from the
> sea, was 1,800 feet in breadth, and the ring of land within it
> the same.... And they covered the whole circuit of the outer-
> most wall with a veneer of bronze.... On the middle of the
> larger island there was a special course for horse-racing. Its
> width was 600 feet and its length that of a complete circuit of
> the island, which was reserved for it. Round it on both sides
> were barracks for the main body of the king's bodyguard.

A more select body of the more trustworthy were stationed on the smaller island ring....[21]

The moat surrounding it was 1,200 feet wide, "and the ring of land again equal to it...."[22] The wall going around this second-largest ring-island was sheeted with tin.

A 600-foot-wide moat encircled the innermost island, 3,000 feet in diameter. At its very center was a wall of gold surrounding the location where, very long ago, Poseidon, god of the sea, lay with a mortal native, Kleito, to engender the ruling lineage of Atlantis. Although entry to this sacred site was forbidden, continuous offerings from far and wide were permitted outside the enclosure. It was located on the royal grounds, where the palace stood. "Each successive king added to its beauties," Plato wrote, "doing his best to surpass his predecessors, until they had made a residence whose size and beauty were astounding to see."[23]

It was eclipsed, however, by a supreme example of Atlantean architecture. The Temple of Poseidon sprawled 600 feet long, was 300 feet wide, and rose 150 feet tall, its exterior covered with sheets of silver. Gold statues of various gods were depicted within the pediment over the entrance. "Inside, the roof was ivory picked out with gold, silver and high-grade copper, and all the walls, pillars and floor were covered with copper sheeting." Around the interior, against the walls, "were statues of the original ten kings and their wives, and many others dedicated by kings and private persons belonging to the city and its dominions."

Near the far end of the temple reared a gold colossus of Poseidon, "so tall that his head almost touched the roof." He was portrayed standing in a chariot pulled by six winged horses, around the base of which were representations of 100 sea-nymphs riding on the backs of dolphins. Ringing these Nereids were "many other statues dedicated by private persons." Before them "there was an altar of a size and workmanship to match that of the building," at the precise center of which stood a copper pillar engraved with the laws of the sea-god together with "an oath invoking awful curses on those who disobeyed" them. Beyond it was a ritual firepit.

Outside the temple,

> two springs, cold and hot, provided an unlimited supply of water for appropriate purposes, remarkable for their agreeable quality and excellence, and this they made available by surrounding the springs with suitable buildings and plantations, leading some of the fresh water into basins, or into covered hot baths. Separate accommodations were provided for royalty and for commoners or women, for horses and other beasts of burden. The outflow was directed into the grove of Poseidon, which, because of the goodness of its soil, was full of trees of marvelous beauty and height, and also channeled the fresh water to the outer ring-islands by aqueducts at the bridges.[24]

Roaming free in the sacred grove were several bulls, one of which was chosen for sacrifice every fifth and sixth year during meetings of the emperor with his nine governors. At the zenith of its fortunes, Atlantis was the world's superpower. It fielded 10,000 two-horse chariots, each one carrying an infantryman and charioteer. An additional 120,000 horses served in the army, with 120,000 hoplites carrying spear and shield, joined by 120,000 archers; 120,000 slingers; 180,000 lightly armed stone throwers; and 180,000 javelin men, all under the command of 60,000 officers. The navy possessed 1,200 warships staffed by 240,000 sailors. Altogether, the Atlantean military comprised 960,000 men at arms. As Plato explained, "there was an unlimited supply of men in the mountains and other parts of the country."[25]

We may roughly deduce from the number of its armed forces personnel—accounting for an average family of two grandparents, two parents, and three children—that the total human population of the island was about 6,720,000. Their enormous military was needed to occupy and control a vast empire, which locally included Madeira, the Canaries, and Azores, westward across the sea to areas of "the opposite continent," as Plato referred to America, and eastward to Iberia and western Italy, across North Africa to the Egyptian border.[26] He stated how this immense power eventually marched into the Eastern Mediterranean World, threatening to conquer the Egyptians and Greeks, who defeated the invaders and turned them back. Thereafter, earthquakes and floods annihilated the victors. "And in a single day and night, the island of Atlantis was similarly swallowed up by the sea and vanished."[27]

These terminal events, according to the temple priest at Sais, took place around 9600 BC. Such remote antiquity is deplored by skeptics of Plato's account as entirely unrealistic. They correctly point out that neither Egyptian kingdoms nor Athens existed at that time, and would not even begin to emerge for another 66 centuries. Nothing remotely resembling the metallurgy, cities, monumental architecture, armies, ships, agriculture, or irrigation projects described by the dialogues was known 11 and a half millennia ago.

Readers favoring a literal interpretation of the *Timaeus* and *Kritias* argue that the island's destruction coincided with the violent close of the last glacial epoch. As such, they conclude that Atlantis was originally an Ice Age civilization. Accepting Plato's date at face value, however, would be equivalent to placing America's Iraq War in the Stone Age. Instead, he explains in the *Timaeus* how Greeks of Solon's generation reckoned "up the generations to calculate how long ago the events in question had taken place," not in our solar years.[28] More to the point, the Egyptians who shared their Atlantis account with visiting Athenians described it in *lunar* time. Accordingly, when they told Solon that the Atlanto-Athenian War occurred 9,000 years earlier, they were telling him that it actually took place around 1200 BC.

If a 10th-millennium-BC Atlantis is problematical in the extreme, a late 13th-century-BC version is a perfect fit, because it parallels the

Late Bronze Age, when all the physical features presented by the *Kritias* attained their florescence. This period was likewise characterized by major military clashes between the Greeks and an otherwise-unidentified power referred to as the *Meshwesh*, or "Sea Peoples," who invaded Egypt, where they were defeated. Archaeo-astronomers, geologists, paleo-botanists and other specialists in related fields also determined that the Bronze Age was abruptly terminated by widespread earthquakes, fires, and floods around 1200 BC.[29]

These contemporaneous natural, archaeological, and cultural features lend persuasive credence to Plato's report and therefore to the historical reality of his Atlantis as both the civilized epitome of the Bronze Age and a victim of the global catastrophe that closed it out.

NOTES

1. "Plato," *Encyclopaedia Britannica*, 2002.
2. Charles Hartshorne, *The Darkness and the Light*, State University of New York Press, 1990, and A.N. Whitehead, *Process and Reality. An Essay in Cosmology. Gifford Lectures Delivered in the University of Edinburgh During the Session 1927–1928*, N.Y.: Macmillan, 1929.
3. David Hatcher Childress, "Quest for Atlantis," IL: *World Explorer*, vol. 1, no. 6, May 1995.
4. *The Commentaries of Proclus on the Timaeus of Plato*, translated by Thomas Taylor, CreateSpace Independent Publishing Platform, 2012.
5. Ibid.
6. Frank Joseph, *The Atlantis Encyclopedia*, N.J.: New Page Books, 2005.
7. L. Sprague De Camp, *Lost Continents*, N.Y.: Dover Publications, 1970.
8. Ivan Lissner, *Dieu Etat Déjà La*, Paris: Bibliotheque Des Grandes Enigmes, 1978.

9. *The Timaeus and the Kritias, or Atlanticus, The Thomas Taylor translation*, Foreword by R. Catesby Taliaferro, Washington, D.C.: Pantheon Books, 1944.

10. Ibid. *Timaeus* 20: 31, 32; and 26: 38; *Kritias* 106: 10.

11. Ibid. *Timaeus* 21: 34.

12. Ibid. *Timaeus* 24: 35.

13. Ibid.

14. Ibid. *Kritias* 114: 9.

15. Ibid. *Kritias* 114: 35.

16. Frank C. Whitmore, Jr., et al, "Elephant Teeth From the Atlantic Continental Shelf," *Science*, 156: 1477–1481, 1967.

17. *The Timaeus and the Kritias, or Atlanticus, The Thomas Taylor translation*, Foreword by R. Catesby Taliaferro, Washington, D.C.: Pantheon Books, 1944: *Kritias* 118: 22.

18. Craig Whitney, "Soviet Scientist Says Ocean Site May Be Atlantis," Special to the *New York Times*, May 20, 1978.

19. *The Timaeus and the Kritias, or Atlanticus, The Thomas Taylor translation*, Foreword by R. Catesby Taliaferro, Washington, D.C.: Pantheon Books, 1944: *Kritias* 118: 5.

20. Ibid. *Kritias* 117: 26.

21. Ibid. *Kritias* 113: 28.

22. Ibid.

23. Ibid. *Kritias* 115: 18.

24. Ibid. *Kritias* 116: 19.

25. Ibid. *Kritias* 4(e).

26. Ibid. *Timaeus* 25: 2.

27. Ibid. *Timaeus* 25: 26.

28. Ibid. *Timaeus* 22: 8.

29. Trevor Palmer and Mark E. Bailey, eds., *Natural Catastrophes During Bronze Age Civilizations: Archaeological, Geological, Astronomical and Cultural Perspectives*, Oxford: Archaeo Press, 1998.

Ancient Cosmologies: The Symbolic Keys to Our True Origins?

By Laird Scranton

China presents some interesting challenges to those who study ancient creation traditions. To begin with, presently there is an enormous gap of knowledge about these traditions due to a lack of surviving evidence. Because of this gap, concepts and practices that date from around 3000 BC are known to us primarily through texts that may not have been written down until around 300 BC; therefore everything that transpired in this time frame is subject to uncertainty and dispute. For example, ancient Chinese traditions honor eight mythical emperors or sages, but depending on which school of thought you embrace, the candidates who were thought to hold those honored titles may vary.

To complicate matters further, while the terminology that is used to describe these creation traditions is generally agreed upon, the actual import of these terms can often be the subject of extended debate. The further back in time we go, the less clear it is whether a given reference should be treated as myth, history, or something in between. For example, there is general agreement that the primordial creator-god of ancient China was named *Fu-Xi* or *Pau-Xi*. However, scholars are uncertain whether this name referred to a mythical deity, a historic individual, a tribe, an emperor, or perhaps even a dynasty of emperors.

My own studies of ancient traditions began in the 1990s with a modern-day African tribe from Mali (in northwest Africa) called the Dogon, whose culture serves as a kind of crossroads for ancient traditions in general. Some Dogon practices align with those of Judaism, some with those of ancient Egypt, and some with those of ancient Buddhism. They are also the keepers of a complex creation tradition that is cast in the familiar symbols of many of the classic ancient creation traditions—the same set of spiraling coils, clay pots, and serpents that Carl Jung identified as archetypes. Study of a modern-day tribe such as the Dogon also offers the advantage of being able to interview living priests who retain a clear understanding their own myths and symbols and are capable of explaining them in modern terms.

Seeing what I considered to be disparate references from several different traditions co-existing side-by-side in Dogon culture suggested to me that ancient religions from various regions of the world might have actually had more in common with one another than is traditionally presumed. And so, using the Dogon symbolic references as a framework, my work over the past 20 years has been to try to identify and correlate various elements that these ancient traditions shared with one another. Often I use evidence that has survived coherently in one tradition to fill in gaps of missing knowledge in other similar traditions. I compare my process to the one that English language scholars employed to successfully reconcile the many variant versions of Shakespeare's plays.

The term *cosmology* refers to concepts of creation and how they are understood by a culture. Historically, concepts of cosmology are understood to have preceded writing in ancient cultures. They seem to have been passed down through oral tradition, couched in symbols, myths, and symbolic acts that were "tagged" to certain civilizing skills, such as the weaving of a cloth or the plowing of a field . From this perspective, symbolism can be seen as the effective language of ancient cosmology. In each of the cultures I have studied, including those of ancient China, there is a overtly stated belief that this cosmology, along with its related civilizing skills, was deliberately instructed (or gifted to humanity) by knowledgeable ancestor-teachers or deities in some remote epoch. Even in ancient Egypt there was an explicit tradition that the written hieroglyphic language was a gift to the ancient Egyptians from their gods.

Symbolism within the cosmologies I study is typically given in relation to three distinct creation themes: the creation of the universe from a cosmic egg, the formation of matter from waves, and the growth of a living being from a fertilized egg. In the Dogon tradition, all three themes are expressed in terms that seem outwardly scientific, using a single set of well-defined symbols. Because of this, each symbol carries a set of parallel meanings that apply respectively to each of the three creational themes. From this viewpoint, the image of a clay pot can represent a particle of matter when applied or linked to one creational theme, but can also represent a womb when applied or linked to another. So whenever we discuss the likely meaning of a given symbol, we first need to place it in context by specifying which creation theme we are discussing.

In ancient Buddhism there was a concept called an *adequate symbol*. This is a type of symbol whose meaning is said to inhere in its form, and so cannot ultimately be lost, even if the meaning is somehow forgotten by the long generational chain of initiates. On reflection, I realized that this could only be the case if the symbol reflected the actual image of something that can be observed in nature. An example of this kind of symbol is the Dogon drawing that probably represents the sub-components of their likely counterpart to an atom. These sub-components are called *sene seeds*; they are the conceptual equivalent of protons, neutrons, and electrons. The Dogon priests say that the sene seeds surround their atom, crossing in all directions to form a kind of a nest, in the same shape as a typical electron orbital pattern.

Ongoing correlations between these ancient cosmologies suggest that they may have all derived from a single common source or parent tradition. As a part of my comparative studies I have evolved a list of what I call *signature signs* of that parent source: words, concepts, references, or practices that I consider to be unique to the tradition, such that their presence in other cultures signals the likely influence of this same cosmology. Conversely, I use this same list of signature practices to proactively predict what I would expect to find in some unstudied culture if they had been influenced by this same tradition.

Several attributes of these ancient traditions have proven to be enormously helpful to my comparative studies. First, I could see that each term of the tradition carries more than one meaning. These meanings are distanced from one another logically, such that simply knowing the first meaning would not reasonably enable a person to guess the secondary meanings. As an example of this, there is a Dogon word, *po,* that refers to the concept of mass or matter, but that can also mean "primeval time." Compare this to the Egyptian hieroglyphic word *pau,* which means "mass, matter, or substance," but also refers to the beginning of time. I realized that these multiple meanings, which are overtly defined within the context of the Dogon creation tradition, provided me with a mechanism by which I could positively correlate words among cultures. I later came to understand that the grouped meanings "float" with the creational concept, not necessarily with a particular phonetic pronunciation, and so served as a means of positive correlation even when the ancient terms I was comparing were given in two different languages.

Based on these comparisons I could see that the Dogon "hidden god" *Amma,* whose name also means "to grasp, hold firm, or establish," was a likely counterpart to the Egyptian "hidden god" *Amen,* whose name also means "to grasp." (I learned that the Hebrew word *Amen* that is pronounced at the end of a prayer also comes from a root that means "to establish.") The name of the Dogon *Sigi* festival (a festival of Sirius that is celebrated every 60 years) was a likely correlate to the Egyptian word *skhai,* which means "to celebrate a festival." A Dogon mythological character named *Ogo,* who plays the role of light in a Dogon creation myth, was a likely counterpart to the Egyptian light god *Aakhu.* Over time I was able to compile a long list of Dogon and Egyptian words that seem to correlate based on matched sets of meanings.

One significant detail that came out of these word comparisons relates to ancient tribes and how they were named. The general term for a group of North African tribes (ancestors to the Berbers) that lived in Egypt prior to the First Dynasty is *amazigh*. One researcher I know, an ethologist named Helene Hagan, who studies these tribes, proposed that the term *amazigh* combined the names of two Egyptian gods: *Amen* and *Asar* (Osiris). My outlook, based on word comparisons, was that the term combined the name of the Dogon god *Amma* with a version of the Dogon/Egyptian word *sigi/skhai*, and so meant "celebrates Amma." In other words, it looked to me as if the tribe had been named for the deity (or aspect of creation) they particularly celebrated, almost similar to the concept of a student who majors in a particular subject in college being called by that major (e.g., he is an English major, she's a biology major, etc.).

From that perspective, there was a priestly tribe I was studying from the high borderland region between Tibet and China called the *Na-Khi* or *Na-Xi*. I knew that the term *Na* meant "mother" in the Dogon language, and that *Nana* was the name of a Neith-like spider that weaves matter in the Dogon tradition. In the context of *Na-Khi*, the word *na* also means "mother." I also verified that the term *Xi* could imply "celebration" in the Na-Khi language. From that perspective it would be reasonable to interpret the name of the tribe as combining the word *Na* and *sigi/skhai*, or "celebrates Na." From there it was fairly easy to determine that an ancient name for Egypt *Mera* can mean "loves Ra," or that an ancient name of the Hebrew tribes *Yahuda* means "praises Yah." And so, working from that perspective I could see, based solely on the outward form of the name, that the Chinese term *Pau-Xi* fits the naming pattern of a priestly tribe associated with this same creation tradition, and that it likely meant "Celebrates the Pau," *Pau* being the final stage of matter in the Dogon/Egyptian cosmology.

The next apparent convention of the tradition that proved helpful to my studies in China relates to commonality of language. My experience while correlating these ancient terms has been that there is a trend toward an increasing similarity of terms the further backward we move in time. I first noted this while exploring possible relationships among the cosmologies I study and the archaic megalithic site at Gobekli Tepe in southeastern Turkey. This site is so exceedingly ancient that it actually pre-dates the earliest evidence we have for many of the tools that would have been required to build it. It also predates the earliest-known written language by nearly 7,000 years.

I learned that there are upwards of 25 different meanings associated with the Turkish word *tepe*, many of which seem consistent with concepts of cosmology. At least a dozen of those same meanings can also be found in an Egyptian hieroglyphic dictionary, expressed in terms of the phonetic root *tep-* or *tepe-*. In other words, I could demonstrate that when the ancient Egyptians used the term *tep, tepe,* or *tepi*, they understood it in the same essential ways as modern-day Turks do, and applied it in ways that relate to the exceedingly ancient Turkish site Gobekli Tepe.

Based on these commonalities, I presumed the Gobekli Tepe site to have had cosmological significance for its builders and inhabitants. I could see that various animals whose carved images appear on megaliths at the site play a well-defined symbolic role in the creation traditions I explore. However, there were certain creatures pictured, such as the scorpion, that held no obvious position in my correlated cosmology. So as a way of sorting out their purpose, I decided to examine the Egyptian hieroglyphic words that reflect their names, hoping to turn up clues as to why they might have been included. I discovered that not just the animals that I considered to be exceptions, but each animal pictured on the Gobekli Tepe megaliths had an Egyptian name that was pronounced like (was essentially a homonym for) a familiar term of cosmology. In other words, it was possible that these images could have represented a kind of proto-writing, whereby a Neolithic hunter/gatherer would see the image of an animal, say its familiar name, and in so doing also speak a term of cosmology. Perhaps he may have even received instruction about the related cosmological concept at that site.

Experiences like these underscored for me the potential that commonality of language might hold for my cross-cultural studies. They also pointed to another helpful attribute of language, which is the tendency of significant words to be retained over very long periods of time within a language. Some traditional linguists refer to these kinds of words as *ultraconserved* words. And so one of the approaches I took to the study of ancient Chinese creation traditions was to compare ancient Chinese terms to comparable words of cosmology found in other cultures. Knowledge of these commonalities of language and of the animal-based symbolism at Gobekli Tepe made my work much easier when exploring concepts that relate to the ancient Chinese Zodiac. The suggestion was that each animal represented a progressive stage of creation. Through comparisons to ancient Egyptian animal names and the symbols used to write them, I was able to make a case for that interpretation.

Using a similar approach, I discovered that from the standpoint of my cosmologies, the alternate name for the Chinese creator-god, which is pronounced *Fu-Xi*, is based on the term *Fu*, which means "four." I also discovered that an ancient Egyptian word for the number "nine" bears a relationship to the phonetic value *Pau*, which is reflected in terms of this same god as *Pau-Xi*. I learned that in China, the number nine relates to foundational concepts of land management and organization. These begin with the nine continents, of which China's locale in Asia was considered to be the center. Similar organizational concepts extended downward all the way to an ancient plan call the *well-field* system. This system defined the fundamental land unit of agriculture in terms of nine square plots of land, arranged three-by-three around a central well. Despite its known modern-day use in some remote countryside locales in China, this system was thought by some researchers to have been a purely theoretical system. However we now know based on our comparative studies that a matching system of the same name that has long been implemented in actual everyday practice stands at the heart of Dogon agriculture.

Paul Wheatley of the University of Chicago tells us in his seminal work *The Pivot of the Four Quarters* that the ground plans of the earliest civic centers in China were defined in terms of four squares, arranged along their sides into a large square that was inscribed inside a circle. However, Wheatley tells us that ancient Chinese textual descriptions of how to arrange the squares are ambiguous, and so the four squares might just as well have been placed corner-to-corner in the shape of a squared cross—and so defined nine square spaces, the same configuration as the agricultural *well-field* system. Together with the surrounding circle, this is the same figure that Sir E.A. Wallis Budge, author of *An Egyptian Hieroglyphic Dictionary*, gives as the Egyptian "town glyph."

The matching Dogon and Buddhist cosmologies I study begin conceptually with an aligned ritual shrine, referred to by the Dogon priests as a *granary* and by the Buddhists as a *stupa*. The plans of these structures evoke a series of matching geometric shapes that are assigned matched symbolism, and that are understood to mimic the processes of creation by which multiplicity emerges from unity. These shrines are aligned to the cardinal points of east, west, north, and south using a rudimentary geometrical process that reflects the motions of the sun. To accomplish this alignment, a stick is placed in the center of a field and a circle drawn around the stick at a radius that measures twice the length of the stick. In both traditions, distances are measured in *cubits*, a cosmological unit of measure that represents the distance from a person's elbow to the tip of the middle finger, or, alternately, the average stride or step of a person.

An initiate to the tradition marks the two longest shadows of the day, in the morning and the evening, that are cast by the stick. These shadows are marked at the points where they intersect the circle, and define the endpoints of a line that, because the sun rises in the east and sets in the west, is automatically oriented along an east-west axis. If this line were to be measured each day throughout the year, it would pass through the stick on two of those days— the two equinoxes—then move progressively farther away from the stick until the date of the next solstice. Looked at in this way, the stick and the circle create an effective sundial that can be used to track the hours of the day, and a calendar by which to mark the seasons of the year.

According to Paul Wheatley, this same method was used to align each of the earliest ritual centers in ancient China, which were contemporaneous with and functioned similarly to the earliest civic centers in ancient Egypt. Wheatley tells us that, based on the work of Walter Fairservis, these ancient cities grew up, not as we might imagine around seaports or centers of commerce or agriculture, but rather around ritual sites. And so the suggestion is that the alignment of these cities might well have been established by the placement of a ritual shrine similar to a Buddhist *stupa*.

Because this circular base plan for the Dogon and Buddhist aligned shrines derives from the motions of the sun as well as the shadows cast by the sun, the circle comes to symbolize the sun in both traditions. Also, because cosmology is understood to have preceded the first evidence of written language in ancient culture, the suggestion is that the shape and traditional meanings of the Egyptian sun glyph (the figure of a circle around a central dot) may have been adapted from this figure. If so, it is easy to see why the sun glyph came to represent the sun, the concept of day, and was associated with other concepts of time. In its earliest form, the ancient Chinese sun glyph took a similar rounded form and represented each of these same concepts.

Although the Dogon have no written language of their own, their creation tradition does include a large number of cosmological images that the Dogon priests draw in the sand with a stick whenever they discuss cosmological concepts. In fact, the priests describe themselves as being incapable of discussing these concepts without also drawing them. Upwards of 30 such Dogon drawings take shapes that seem outwardly similar to Egyptian glyphs. Because each of the Dogon drawings represents a specific concept, I began to wonder what the result might be if I were to substitute the Dogon concepts for the similar shapes when I found them in ancient Egyptian words, in much the same way that one would solve a Rebus puzzle. What I found was that the concepts created a kind of symbolic sentence that, when read together, seemed to define the meaning of the Egyptian word.

Perhaps the most accessible example of this substitutional method of reading is found in an Egyptian word *met,* which means "week." This word is written with only two glyphs: the circular sun glyph and an upside-down U figure that represents the Egyptian number 10. Looking at the word, I realized that it could be interpreted symbolically to mean "10 days," which was the actual definition of an ancient Egyptian week. That insight led me to wonder whether the symbols of other Egyptian cosmological words might possibly work in a similar way. With a little effort I soon discovered that apparently they all do! I began my search for similar constructions by looking to other Egyptian words whose meanings relate to periods of time. In each case, there was a reasonable perspective from which the symbolic glyph/concepts could be seen to define each word's meaning.

Based on my experiences with ancient Egyptian language, one of the first hieroglyphic words I chose to focus on during my studies of ancient Chinese cosmology was the Chinese word for "week." I discovered that it, too, was written with only two glyphs: the Chinese sun glyph, and the Chinese number 10. The ancient Chinese calendar was based on the same fundamental units of time as those in ancient

Egypt, including a 360-day year, a 30-day month, and a 10-day week; just as the Egyptian word *met* did, I could see that this Chinese word defined their ancient week symbolically. However, linguists in China have interpreted the symbols of the word to mean "10 suns," not "10 days." This may be due to the storyline of an ancient Chinese myth that tells of an archer who shoots nine of 10 suns from the branches of a mythical mulberry tree. Like the traditional researchers in Egypt, these linguists somehow never conceived of the word as a literal definition of a 10-day week.

Based on just the few examples cited so far, it became apparent to me that fundamental similarities existed between the symbolic traditions in ancient China and those that were familiar to me from ancient Egypt and the Dogon. This view was upheld as I pursued each signature element of my comparative cosmological plan in relation to ancient China. Likewise, I came to understand that when considering their earliest forms, I could use the definitions of Dogon and Egyptian words and symbols to help clarify the meanings of certain poorly understood concepts in ancient China.

One of these very early concepts of ancient China is the notion of the *yijing* or *I-Ching*. Another helpful feature of the cosmologies I study is that many of its words seem to have been formulated by mixing and matching a well-defined set of phonetic prefixes and suffixes to create larger words. For example, I knew that the term *nu* referred to "primordial waves or water," and that *ma* meant "to examine or perceive." So it was not surprising to me that the Egyptian term *nu maa* (comparable to the Dogon term *nummo*) referred to the cosmological concept of "waves perceived."

In China, the term *yijing* was traditionally understood to combine the two root phonemes *yi* and *jing*. The term *yi* is commonly translated as "changes," but several of my sources on Chinese cosmology insisted that it more properly referred to concept of change in the singular. Cross-checking to my Dogon and Egyptian dictionaries, I found comparable terms that were defined to mean "a change in state," similar to what happens to water when it freezes to become ice, or boils to produce water vapor. One Dogon reference compared this concept of change to the process of gelatin jelling. The Dogon words were given in the context of changes that are said to occur with matter in its primordial, wavelike state as it begins its transformation into particles.

The second Chinese phoneme *jing* was understood to refer to a complex concept of vibration, turning, and twisting. Based on my knowledge of cosmology I could see that it likely referred to the raising up and twisting of matter that is also said to happen after a wave is perceived. But I was uncertain how to characterize that motion until I looked to a similar term that is defined in the Dogon dictionary. Genevieve Calame-Griaule, the French anthropologist who compiled the dictionary, chose to include a diagram in her dictionary to illustrate the concept. It depicts a counter-weighted bar that balances on a pivot-point and that, according to Calame-Griaule, defines a pivoting motion. In other words, the very same concept that Paul Wheatley chose as a title to define his study of ancient China, *The Pivot of the Four Quarters*.

These kinds of comparative techniques demonstrate ways in which many of the classic creation traditions are fundamentally similar to one another. So far, over the course of four books, the process of my research has been largely geographic, moving from West Africa to Egypt, then to India and Tibet, and now to ancient China. While the comparisons between cultures tend to clarify things like the meanings of symbols, words, myths, or rituals, and help define the contours of what resembles a designed system of cosmology, they also provide important clues to a likely common point of origin for that system. My ultimate hope is that this information will make it possible to trace a coherent path of development forward from some as-yet-unidentified archaic culture to each of these other classic creation traditions.

BIBLIOGRAPHY

Allan, Sarah. *The Shape of the Turtle: Myth Art and Cosmos in Early China.* Albany, N.Y.: State University of New York Press, 1991.

Budge, E.A. Wallis. *An Egyptian Hierglyphic Dictionary.* Mineola, N.Y.: Dover Publications, Inc., 1978.

Cai Yanxin. *Chinese Ancient Cities: The Grid System, Feng Shui, and Il Fong. http://landsofwisdom.com/?p=3491.*

Calame-Griaule, Genevieve. *Dictionnaire Dogon.* Paris: Librarie C. Klincksieck.

Griaule, Marcel. *Conversations With Ogotemmeli.* Oxford University Press, 1970.

Griaule, Marcel and Germaine Dieterlen. *The Pale Fox.* Paris: Continuum Foundation, 1986.

Hagan, Helene. *The Shining Ones: An Entymological Essay on the Amazigh Roots of Egyptian Civilization.* Xlibris, 2000.

Lewis, Mark Edward. *The Construction of Space in Early China.* Albany, N.Y.: State University of New York Press, 2006.

Mathieu, Christine. *A History and Anthropological Study of the Ancient Kingdoms of the Sino-Tibetan Borderland—Naxi and Mosuo.* Lewiston, Australia: The Edwin Mellen Press, 2003.

Milnor, Seaver Johnson. "A Comparison Between the Development of the Chinese Writing System and Dongba Pictographs." Seattle, Wash.: *University of Washington Working Papers in Linguistics,* Vol. 24 (2005), eds. Daniel J. Jinguji and Steven Moran, pp 30-45: *http://depts.washington.edu/uwwpl/vol24/pub_submission_Milnor.pdf.*

Rosemont, Jr., Henry. *Explorations in Early Chinese Cosmology.* Chico, Calif.: Scholars Press, 2006.

Smith, Richard. *Fathoming the Cosmos and Ordering the World: The Yijing (I-Ching, or Classic of Changes) and its Evolution in China.* Charlottesville, Va: University of Virginia Press, 1999.

Snodgrass, Adrian. *Architecture, Time and Eternity.* Delhi, India: Aditya Prakashan, 1990.

———. *The Symbolism of the Stupa.* Delhi, India: Motilal Banarsidass Publishers, 1992.

Wheatley, Paul. *The Pivot of the Four Quarters: A Preliminary Enquiry Into the Origins and Character of the Ancient Chinese City.* Chicago, Ill.: Aldine Publishing Company, 1971.

Worshiping the Three Sage Kings and Five Virtuous Emperors. Beijing: Foreign Languages Press, 2007.

TO THE WEST, THE LARGEST: GIANTS IN NATIVE AMERICAN MYTH AND FOLKLORE

BY MICAH HANKS

In the eastern regions of this modern land of providence and prosperity, in what is current-day Tennessee and North Carolina, there remains an ancient and hilly region, with parts almost forgotten, that shelters the stuff of myth and imagination. Within its cavernous hills, one will find tales of all the great, fabled, and legendary beings of yore—strange folk who seem to traverse the boundaries between the extraordinary and the everyday, haunting the moist and mossy floors of evergreen forests whose treetops extend high enough into the mountain air to kiss the moving clouds with the bristly tips of their cones.

There are tales throughout this region of ancient tribes whose large-eyed kinsmen existed only by pale moonlight. In equal measure, there are rumors of vast and sprawling underground fortresses that are inhabited—and fiercely guarded—by inhuman creatures. And of course, there are the famous stories of strange, haunting illuminations that lift right from the tops of stony crags that line the mountain ridges, and carry themselves into the night air like great glowing fireflies, fluttering their unseen wings against the oncoming breeze.

The kinds of stories described here, based on Native American legends, frontier folklore, and strange rumors carried along through the ages, border on the otherworldly. At times, they might resemble similar fantastic tales of other locales, namely that of European fairy lore, which served as inspiration for the likes of J.R.R. Tolkien, who would use such mythology as fodder in crafting a new mythic interpretation of the roots of Western civilization. Without contest, this strange realm of fantasy that Tolkien bore from his fertile imagination is among the most well-known and loved fantasy landscapes today. The incredible adventures he offered us, replete with dwarves, elves, goblins, and wizards, have become staples of both modern literature and entertainment, intricately woven around the influence of a curious little circular band of gold, crafted out of fire and sorcery, whose wicked influence could command entire armies.

Few would look at America and ever consider it any likeness to Tolkien's aforementioned fantasies. The United States today is a land of convenience, at very best, and a place where the longing for worlds apart from our own, inhabited by beings unlike modern people, is relegated solely to fiction works such as *The Lord of the Rings.* This, however, was not always the case, as evidenced by those incredible legends of yesteryear, carried along almost entirely by spoken tradition, and based on memories of people who lived here long ago, and far earlier than those privy to the same European folklore that bore Tolkien's legacy. These Native American legends tell of small people, like Tolkien's hobbits, who reside within holes in the ground, the likes of which no living person has entered to tell whether they offer, as Tolkien himself suggested, "oozy smells and the ends of worms," or the comfort of a well-kept underground residence. But perhaps there are other beings the ancient Americans remembered, too, which similarly found their way into those fantastic narratives Tolkien wove together in the late evenings from his study, crafting letters, maps, and illustrations amid a haze of Dunhill tobacco smoke rising from the bowl of his pipe. For as much as the little folk took the center stage in those tales, there had been mention of another archetypal non-human that would frequent the landscape of both his fantasy realm, and that of the ancient Americas, as well. These were the giants, beings of massive size, strength, and influence who once were said to live among us.

The Americas are riddled with the scratches and etchings of many a traveler to have come and gone amidst their rocky hills and hollows. These carvings in stone—or *petroglyphs*—span thousands of years, as culture upon culture have traversed our haunted landscape in search of whatever secrets its imposing granite walls and canyons may have kept hidden. In such markings, we occasionally find clues to a reality that may have existed before us—evidence of those who once forged their path through the region and chose to leave their mark upon it. Whether they passed through this land unscathed or not, it could be argued that the land must have left its unrepentant mark on *them*.

It is in one famous stone marking of this sort, chiseled into a massive boulder that lies in a cornfield between two high mountain ridges of western North Carolina, that an odd connection to the strange and gigantic folk that Native American legends have helped us remember begins to emerge. The Judaculla Old Fields, as 19th-century anthropologist James Mooney wrote of the place, lay "about the head of Tuckasegee river, in Jackson, North Carolina."[1] There, along the country outskirts of a modest community called Webster, just outside the college town of Cullowhee, "is one large rock bearing numerous petroglyphs, rings, cup-shaped depressions, [and] fishbone patterns."[2] The rock to which Mooney refers, known today as Judaculla Rock, tells a most unique story, for its name is drawn from the corrupted pronunciation of an earlier Cherokee Indian word, *Tsul 'kalu*, the name given to their legendary god of the hunt.

Tsul 'kalu is of particular interest among such legends, because he appears to be only one among a scant few references to giant folk in Cherokee mythology. The name has a peculiar meaning, as it translates to literally describe "slanting eyes" or "he who has them slanting."[3] Tsul 'kalu, thus, was envisioned by the ancient Cherokee as a slant-eyed giant, and ruler of the game that they relied on for sustenance.

The legend of Tsul 'kalu begins long ago, near a Cherokee town called Kanuga on the Pigeon River. A young woman who had not yet married was advised by her mother to wed a skilled hunter, so that they would never be for want. Soon, a man came to her late in the evening, and while he would visit her by cover of darkness, this mysterious hunter would always leave before daylight, despite bringing plenty of venison and firewood for the girl and her mother, who finally pleaded with her daughter to convince him to stay long enough so that she could meet him. He agreed while visiting the following evening that he would stay until morning light could illuminate his figure, but only if the girl's mother would honor his sole request: that she not be frightened, or call him ugly once she had seen him.

The following morning, the girl's mother came to meet the man her daughter had spoken of with such fondness, with equal hope that they would marry. As she entered her daughter's room within the hut, she discovered that the mysterious evening hunter to become her beau was a strange-looking man of enormous size. Among his peculiar features, this man also bore strange, slanting eyes, which had only just begun to open with wakefulness. Seeing this giant beginning to rise from his slumber, the old woman ran from the house screaming, which angered the drowsy Tsul 'kalu, who snatched up his new wife, and together they left for the western lands where the curious giant had made his home.

Once Tsul 'kalu and his wife were gone, the girl's family became saddened by her disappearance. Thus, her brother decided to pursue the newlyweds, following their spoor in the soft earth, along with new, smaller footprints that made apparent to him that he was now an uncle. The path Tsul 'kalu's new family had left as they traveled eventually led the young man to a large stone lair extending far back into a stony mountain ridge. There within the cave he could see many people dancing, including his sister, who came and spoke to him but would not leave the place, despite there being no sign of her mysterious and gigantic suitor. Frustrated, the brother finally left the cave, his sister remaining behind with the as-yet-unseen giant.

The family continued on in her absence back at Kanuga, with only an occasional thought of the daughter who left them. However, to their great surprise, one day the girl returned to the home of her mother, telling her family that she and Tsul 'kalu had been hunting in the area, and that if they wished to meet him, they should visit their encampment early the following morning. They agreed, and the family arose before sunrise the following day, again eager to meet the giant husband of their beloved family member. By the time they arrived, the camp they found had been abandoned, save for a plentiful offering of deer killed the previous night, providing enough venison for all the villagers of Kanuga to feast upon. But even this large dinner had not been satisfactory for the girl's brother, who by now had grown increasingly curious about the giant his sister had chosen to live with. He returned again to Tsul 'kalu's cave, making the long journey to the west where their home in the mountainside had been. Upon arriving, a disembodied voice advised him that if he and his people would commit to fasting for seven days, they could be allowed to finally witness him, once and for all, during a visit to their home in Kanuga.

With news of the visit, the fasting ensued among the villagers of Kanuga; however, one foreigner who had been staying in the village lacked the enthusiasm his hosts seemed to share for this long-awaited meeting, and so he would sneak out in the evenings to find food, in defiance of the fast. Once the seventh day arrived, the people of Kanuga, despite their hunger, eagerly awaited Tsul 'kalu's arrival, and began to gather with anticipation as the sounds of a great bellowing began to echo down through the valley, from the direction of the Tennessee mountains to the west. As this rumbling drew closer, the villagers knew that it was Tsul 'kalu approaching. However, the foreigner who had broken the fast had grown increasingly terrified at the great thundering calls of Tsul 'kalu; fearing retribution, he ran from the village, shouting the war cry. This greatly angered Tsul 'kalu, who once gain forbade the people of Kanuga to look upon him, despite further appeals from his young brother-in-law.[4]

The legend pertaining to Tsul 'kalu related here is one of only two primary legends in the Cherokee mythology that feature giants. The second actually bears a number of similarities to the Tsul 'kalu myth. James Mooney cites this second legend in his seminal work *Myths of the Cherokee*, based on a report that appeared in the Nineteenth Annual Report of the Bureau of American Ethnology 1897–98. During his cultural studies of the Cherokee, Mooney had spoken with an elderly man named James Wafford, whose nickname, based on his western Cherokee heritage, was *Tsuskwanun'nawa'ta*, meaning "worn-out blanket." Wafford shared with Mooney a compelling retelling of a much older native legend, which had been passed to him by his grandmother sometime in the early 19th century:

James Wafford, who was born in Georgia in 1806, said that his grandmother, who must have been born about the middle of the previous century, told him that she had heard from the old people that long before her time, a party of giants had come once to visit the Cherokee. They were nearly twice as tall as common men, and had their eyes set slanting in their heads, so that the Cherokee called them Tsunil'kälû', the "slant-eyed people," because they resembled the giant hunter Tsul 'kalu. They said that these giants lived very far away, in the direction in which the sun goes down. The Cherokee received them as friends, and they stayed some time, and then returned to their home in the west. The story may be a distorted historical tradition.[5]

The stories of Tsul 'kalu and the giants who visited the Cherokee in Wafford's legend have fueled speculation about whether, as Mooney suggested, there could be some factual basis behind these myths. What might have been the source of this "cultural tradition" that Mooney speculated about? Perhaps more importantly, are there other instances where legends of giants might corroborate with the kinds of tales Mooney collected?

The modern popularity that has been afforded subjects such as Sasquatch or Bigfoot, a legendary humanlike but primitive beast that supposedly exists in remote portions of the United States, have only fueled such speculation. Tenuous links could, and have, been implied that link the Tsul 'kalu myths with the possible real existence of Sasquatches, given the consideration that the giants of Cherokee tradition might be a single instance among a broader "wild man" mythology spanning several indigenous cultures. But there are perhaps more compelling legends that could be evoked for comparison with the sparring references to giants in Cherokee lore, which may have born such ideas as the existence of literal giants that roamed the ancient Americas.

MORE GIANTS, FURTHER WEST

Another famous legend about giants among Native American groups involves a race of beings known as the Si-Te-Cah, which were believed to be cannibalistic giants with red hair, as told of in the legends of the Paiute people of Nevada and surrounding western states. This legend is a strange one, made particularly striking due in part to the fact that, unlike the Cherokee legends of giants from the west, the Si-Te-Cah legend bears a modern component that lends some credence to the story.

The story of the Si-Te-Cah begins as a folktale about a group of giant, red-haired cannibals who had once lived as a rival tribe to the Paiute. Their barbaric behavior culminated in a battle in which the Si-Te-Cah were driven into a cave by the Paiute, who built a large fire at the entrance of the cavern, killing the cannibals trapped inside.[6] This story by itself might have remained but another legend among native tribes, had it not been for the discovery of actual skeletons in a cave named for the nearby town of Lovelock, Nevada. Beginning in 1911, guano miners began unearthing partially mummified human remains, along with a host of artifacts, which had been buried and preserved within several feet of guano on the cave's floor. It would be another year before authorities were notified of the discoveries. Perhaps the reason for the wait was simply that the miners hadn't wanted to interrupt their operation, and thus withheld any information that might have prevented them from continuing their work. However, by the time archaeologists had been able to access the site, a number of precious artifacts had been destroyed while guano had been harvested. Despite this, a collection of well-preserved artifacts numbering in the thousands survived.[7]

The bodies found among relics in the Lovelock Cave were described as being quite tall in some instances—perhaps as tall as 6 1/2 feet—and with red hair on their heads, just as the Paiute legends had described. But were they really large enough to qualify as giants? There are a number of conflicting opinions on this, one being the supposition that the giant story had purely been a marketing ploy on part of several entrepreneurs in the region who planned to promote their stake in the mystery to legendary status simply to garner tourist interest. However, a series of articles appearing in the Sunday edition of the Reno-based *Nevada State Journal* during the early 1950s made mention of large, 15-inch sandals that were recovered among the artifacts brought out of Lovelock Cave. Such large footwear, one might presume, would also require a large foot on behalf of the one wearing it.[8]

While there exists compelling evidence that Lovelock Cave mummies were of large stature, it remains a difficult case to make for these people being literal "giants." The greatest impediment to this conclusion remains in the fact that the bodies discovered were in many cases destroyed; one of the best-preserved specimens had famously been obtained by an area fraternity, members of which allegedly destroyed it as part of an initiation ceremony.[9] Whether or not this is indeed a true retelling of the fate of one of the Lovelock giants, it does little to aid the true determination of what these bodies are meant to represent with regard to ancient American history. Rumor and hearsay certainly cannot substantiate the assertions any better.

Interestingly, what does appear to have some archaeological evidence to support it is the assertion of cannibalism, often espoused in the Paiute legends regarding the Si-Te-Cah. During the primary excavation that occurred at Lovelock Cave in 1924, evidence of human bones that had been broken open to gain access to the marrow were found in three instances, which archaeologists presumed may have been evidence of actual cannibalism that occurred during a period of famine.[10] And yet, rather ironically, the name *Si-Te-Cah*, when translated, literally means "tule-eaters," in reference to an aquatic plant of which these beings were supposed to frequently partake—hardly the stuff a presumed cannibal of any regular dietary choosing would wish to feast on.

The Case for "Real" Giants

In modern times it has often been asserted that numerous other cases similar to that of the Lovelock giants exist, where the remains of strange bodies, often of very large stature, have been discovered. More often than not in such instances, while human remains bearing these anomalous qualities have been recovered, allegations persist that state that the reports of these findings have been protected or even silenced in some way. Such cases include discoveries that appeared in the writing and letters of Scottish zoologist Ivan T. Sanderson, who had inquired about the unearthing of several large skeletons bearing strange features on the Aleutian island of Shemya during the 1940s. Namely, Sanderson had asked, as many have done since, why there was an apparent record of the Smithsonian Institute obtaining remains that were uncovered, but then apparently losing track of where these seemingly extraordinary discoveries were kept.[11]

In fact, if one digs deeply enough, there are plenty of academic articles, newspaper items, and other references—perhaps numbering in the hundreds or even thousands—that have appeared over the years that detail the discovery of exceptionally large skeletal remains. It is an equally consistent element to this mythos that organizations such as the Smithsonian have appeared and confiscated those remains, and that because there are no books being published or museums being erected to showcase these incredible discoveries, that there must be a conspiracy behind the silence that surrounds the issue. With little doubt, if clear evidence of giants in our midst long ago were to be made publicly known, it would do much to shake the otherwise-firm foundations of modern science, and the disciplines of anthropology and archaeology might radically change upon having to accept that our present understanding of the fossil record and human evolution may have been, up until now at least, fundamentally flawed. This very train of thought had no doubt evoked the criticisms of Ivan Sanderson, who wondered of it was simply a matter of these people being "unable to face rewriting all the textbooks."[12]

Without question there have been instances in which portions of "anomalous" human remains have appeared to go missing, or have simply not been collected and catalogued in a clear and effective manner. Sanderson was correct (along with many others who followed) in asking why these discoveries weren't readily available, or at least easily able to be sourced for future study. However, rather than this being a case of lost or deliberately obfuscated information, perhaps researchers just didn't (and still don't) know where to look. Indeed, several items relating to so-called giant skeletons, despite the conspiracy theories that persist, do still exist in the Smithsonian archives, and public record for these is still available. Notable specimens include what are called the Graham and Chittenden skulls, as well as an alleged "giant" Indian jawbone known as the DeHart jaw, all of which are acknowledged and recorded as extant in the Smithsonian Institute's offsite storage facility, according to the Smithsonian's own accession card catalogue. Additionally, there are clear references made to the discovery of large bones that appear in the annual reports from the Bureau of Ethnology to the Secretary of the Smithsonian, particularly those appearing toward the end of the 19th century, when a number of large skeletons were found.[13] So if these discoveries are not only known to exist, but are also acknowledged by the Smithsonian Institute, is this the final proof that there were indeed giants that roamed the ancient Americas, and thus proving that stories the likes of which appeared in the ancient Cherokee legends may have a factual basis?

The answer is both yes and no—though many, no doubt, would prefer to leave it at a simple, flat, and resounding *no*. What cannot be questioned is that a number of very large human skeletons have been uncovered in parts of the United States and other locales worldwide. Both anecdotal and academic information pertaining to a number of these finds will often assert that the remains bear strange or anomalous features, including misshapen or mutilated skulls (especially those resulting from *trepanning*, in which holes are carved or drilled into the skull itself, a strange practice common to a number of ancient cultures). Altogether, such accounts do seem to present a curious perspective on various aspects of life in the ancient Americas, which do not appear to be quite in keeping with the time line and human ancestry that is generally accepted today.

However, because of the extraordinary nature of such discoveries, it is quite obvious that a number of researchers over the years have allowed their minds to run wild with the possibilities presented by the appearance of what would seem to be anomalous human remains, some even going so far as to suggest that, rather than being human, they were an altogether separate race of large beings that existed apart from people. These ideas, while not backed by scientific data, remain quite popular, and are often further linked to ideas that incorporate alleged paleo contact between humanity and extraterrestrials, and/or supposed demigods that are said to have ascended to Earth to interact and even interbreed with humanity. As a result, the debate regarding large skeletons—whether or not one chooses to call them *giants*—has become so terribly polarized that the subject is seldom given any reasonable objective thought or inquiry; in other words, the mere assertion that records for these finds are known to exist is downplayed entirely by ideological skeptics, who would maintain that strangely large remains of humans are in no way anomalous. Furthermore, to make assertions to the contrary is tantamount to acknowledging they represent a race of monstrous alien beings, rather than humans that bore peculiar traits that were indeed both anomalous *and* worthy of serious scientific study. As with all subjects, there appears to be intellectual middle ground between the ideological extremes that present a road less traveled, which also is capable of providing safe passage for both logical thought and the expansion of awareness about our natural world. One need not look at "giant" skeletons as being something beyond the normal or natural in order to admit to the fascination they inspire, and the questions they present about the order and evolution of the human race.

So what of the Native American legends, then, that tell of the ancient people of this Earth and the mysterious and outsized "others" with whom they crossed paths? The modern mind is all too quick to draw firm distinctions between the real world of our waking existence, and the pure fantasy that the fictional realm may offer. It can be said with certainty that there are clear points that separate what we call *reality* from the musings of the mind that the gifted writers among us occasionally commit to paper for future generations to enjoy. However, we must also be reminded that all such things that exist in fiction, perhaps even the giant folk who appear in both our modern folklore and ancient fairytales, nonetheless have their genesis in this sober reality of ours, at least to some degree.

The inspiration for all such things we separate from our daily lives as being mere fantasy will always come from reality, from real-life experiences, particularly those taken from the more challenging periods in the history of the human race. It may even be true that during periods of territorial dispute and times of conflict, the ancient Americans came up against warriors of rival tribes who were of indeed very large, and who, by virtue of their physical strength and prowess, were both honored and remembered by the people who knew them as foes, not to mention those who comprised their kindred. It would not take a monstrous, inhuman being, or even a giant, perhaps, for the legend of these people to become indelibly caught up in the mythic web of our ancient past: one part retelling of true events, and another part pure embellishment for sake of entertainment and narrative appeal. The result, of course, becomes something that is forever remembered as greater even than the gigantic individuals themselves actually were in their lifetimes.

NOTES

1. Mooney, James. *Myths of the Cherokee*. Mineola, N.Y.: Dover Publications, 1996 (new edition).
2. *www.fs.usda.gov/detail/nfsnc/learning/history-culture/?cid=stelprdb5209557*.
3. Mooney. *Myths of the Cherokee*.
4. Ibid.
5. Ibid.
6. Mayor, Adrienne. *Fossil Legends of the First Americans*. Princeton, N.J.: Princeton University Press, 2005.
7. Loud, Llewellyn, and M. Harrington. "Lovelock Cave." *University of California Publications in American Archaeology and Ethnology*. University of California–Berkeley, February 15, 1929.
8. *Nevada State Journal*. Reno, Nev.. Sunday, February 22, 1953.
9. Llewellyn and Harrington. "Lovelock Cave."
10. Ibid.
11. "Island of Shemya, Alaska." Online article, accessed November 20, 2013: *http://greaterancestors.com/island-of-shemya-alaska/*.

12. Ibid.

13. Hanks, Micah. "Big Buried Secrets: Giant Skeletons and the Smithsonian." July 31, 2013: *http://micahhanks.com/conspiracy-2/big-buried-secrets-giant-skeletons-and-the-smithsonian/*.

WE ARE THE ALIENS

BY PAUL VON WARD

Almost all ancient cultures, including Hindu, Sumerian, Egyptian, and Chinese cultures, told stories and created artwork and artifacts that represented alleged contact with aliens from the skies thousands of years ago. Most modern people conceptualize aliens as the small gray beings that were found in the desert near Roswell, New Mexico, in 1947. Other popular representations range from the fearsome reptilians to Nordic types that could be our half-siblings.

The word *alien* is used as either noun or adjective. As an adjective, it can denote something strange, foreign, or unfamiliar, or someone who was born elsewhere. As a noun, it designates any life-form with origins/genetic roots in another planet. However, given the universe as we know it, I believe that the use of the word *alien* to separate humans from other advanced species can no longer be considered accurate. This is because most of the aliens inhabiting planet Earth right now are human beings. Yes, we are the aliens.

Astronomers now believe that billions of planets throughout our universe are likely to have resources and conditions sufficiently similar to those of Earth to produce intelligent life. But, afraid of shaking up both major religions and Darwinism, they minimize the odds of life "out there" that is more advanced than our own. That said, researchers in the fields of physics, biology, and chemistry suggest that the principles that nurture life on Earth are universal. We humans on planet Earth do not hold a monopoly on life. Given the relatively young age of our planet, it would be foolish to think we are leading the way in the development of consciousness, intelligence, and technology. Indeed, we are still incapable of discerning the presence of other beings if they have hidden themselves using "cloaking technology"—an ability we do not yet have.

Given all this, science in the 21st century should be pointing toward two new hypotheses: one, that highly advanced beings (ABs), far beyond us in knowledge of the universe, have colonized and still are colonizing our planet; and two, that humans have some genes in common with these aliens. These hypotheses lead us in the direction of what I call the advanced being intervention theory (AB-IT). In fact, persuasive evidence described in books by this author[1] and others in this anthology suggests that such ABs have already had a significant impact on human history, and have already visited Earth during several discrete periods throughout history, including the present day. This essay discusses how tangible and credible evidence found in multiple locations and from disparate time periods demonstrates how modern humans came to have genetic links with an unearthly species. Given such evidence, we can no longer claim to be the sole native citizens of Earth. We humans must now place ourselves under the rubric of *alien*.

A Genetic Puzzle

Is it possible to prove that humans share AB genes? First, we know that complex genetic shifts, through accidental or environmentally based mutations, take a very long time. Second, we know that the history of *Homo sapiens sapiens* has fossil gaps and inexplicable quick mutations—quite different from all other species on Earth. Such seemingly instantaneous mutations require an explanation other than the "magical wand" espoused by supernatural religions.

The AB-IT is based on tangible evidence from different periods and events in human evolution that cannot be explained by the present "official" history of the human race. One category of evidence includes anomalous physical characteristics, which are rooted in the human genome. Examples are height and limb proportions; skin, hair, and eye color; and longevity. All of these traits are controlled by the human genome. In cultures of the Abrahamic religious tradition, a very well-known account of such evidence is found in the Dead Sea scrolls.[2] It goes something like this: When Noah was born, his father, Lameck, was alarmed at his strange physical appearance. In that period the proto-Hebrews were aware that a group of ABs maintained surveillance over their tribe. In their language of that era, they labeled these beings as their Watchers—the Nephilim.

So Lameck went to his father, Methuselah, and told him of his concerns about Noah's blue eyes, curly reddish hair, and pale white skin—all uncharacteristic for their tribe. Methuselah then went to Enoch, who went to his father, Jared. Alleged then to be 600 years old, Jared responded that, in his youth, ABs from the sky came down to earth and seduced the daughters of men. This story could not have assuaged Lameck's fears. However, Noah allegedly survived the 11,500 BP cataclysm[3] and lived for 950 years. He added his half-AB genes to his progeny, producing generations of AB-human hybrids. They then apparently seeded this DNA among leading families of the proto-Hebrews and Hyksos in the Near East. Consequently, later generations with partial Watcher genomes likely mixed with groups of *Homo sapiens* elsewhere in the world. These "Noah-like" features have been identified in the rulers of several regions in the premodern world. These families date from both before and after the cataclysm. Similar accounts of ABs interbreeding with "daughters of men" are also found in Egyptian traditions. A long series of Egyptian rulers reportedly had light skin and small stature as a result of a mixed genealogy. As well, similar Aboriginal stories exist on several continents.

AB-IT METHODOLOGY

Given this robust body of evidence, Noah's tale can be used to illustrate a logical and reliable scientific methodology that can be used by researchers to evaluate potential AB-IT cases. Its procedures can be used to develop reasonable counters to skeptical challenges. They force researchers to be clear about what they think happened and to demonstrate why they have a solid basis for their claims.

Proving AB manipulation in the evolution of our ancestors requires at least four stages. The first is *identification of historical clues contained in reports* (words or images) from earlier humans that describe their interactions with nonhumans. The next is a *search for relevant and tangible evidence* that supports the historical story and its clues. Sometimes different types of evidence lead to varying explanations for the theory. Evidence that appears to undermine the hypothesis must be examined. Third, different areas of evidence must be assessed and compared to determine which is the most plausible. This process, with simple and direct logic, must demonstrate a reasonable expectation that further research will support the AB thesis. The final step must then determine if contradictory evidence exists that can nullify the best explanation. This means the null hypothesis, called X, would have to prove that AB intervention could *not* be responsible for the AB-IT evidence. If we desire more credibility, these four steps are necessary in evaluating the areas of alien evidence in this book and others. Examples in this essay include research that involves gigantic aberrations found in human-like skulls and skeleton fossils. Another area is reportedly extremely long lifespans among groups of pre-cataclysmic humans.

First, let's test the thesis that Noah's strange features described prior could have been the result of genetic mutations that involved sexual intercourse with more advanced beings. Using the four-step process, we must be meticulous in describing the evidence and clear about the logic used to assess it.

SKIN, HAIR, AND EYE COLOR

Clues: Similar stories to that described in the Hebrew tale of Noah exist in many cultures and languages, suggesting that his circumstances reflect multiple-culture experiences. The Persians have their version, with a Zal/Sham pair, and the Chinese report that Lao-Tze was born with white hair. They also relate the same peculiar physical features to AB origins. The written records and oral traditions make it clear that such lighter hair, eyes, and skin were exceptions to the normal dark features of all other humans of that era.

Evidence: Extended families with the same exotic features were later identified among early Europeans, Polynesians, Mayans, and other North and Southern Americans. Ancient traditions described them as more knowledgeable and skilled than other humans at the time. Some groups of these seemingly superior humans were very small, almost pygmy-sized, rather than the 4- to 5-feet average height of humans at the time.

Anthropologist and author Susan B. Martinez[4] has amassed impregnable evidence of these exceptional ancestors of modern-day humans. When 16th-century European explorers invaded the Andes they found small groups of pale-skinned people with blond/reddish hair and blue eyes. These strange people seemed to be more intelligent than the natives, but the Spanish conquistadors, who were looking for gold and slaves, massacred them. Indigenous traditions considered these murdered people as a superior caste who were rulers in much earlier civilizations.

People with similarly unexpected physical features were discovered in several other areas of South America by other explorers. There was the bearded, Caucasian race around Lake Titicaca in Bolivia, and the blond, light-skinned natives in the Inca regions of Peru[5] and Chile. Similar pale-skinned people at one time lived in Venezuela (interestingly, in a village called Atlan—as in Atlantis). Another settlement, similarly named, was inhabited by a pale-skinned people in Panama. Other such people were reportedly found on Caribbean islands and in Surinam. The families bearing such features stood out from the general population and in fact were often considered members of a royal line descended from earlier ABs. A historical review of relevant documents, ancient mummies, and art suggests that these "Noahs" were often found in leadership roles in different cultures and regions of the globe.

Comparisons: One hypothesis[6] has been publicly offered as an explanation for the Noah light skin/eye/hair syndrome. It claims albinism, necessarily started by a singular genetic mutation, is the origin of all Caucasian *Homo sapiens*. However, albinism is an genetic condition that runs through all racial groups, not just the roots of a single race. Moreover, only a small percentage of all people are albinism carriers. With one flawed gene, 50 percent of these apparently normal individuals can pass it on, but it takes two carriers— both parents bearing this gene—to produce a child with albinism. In such cases the odds of conceiving a child with albinism are one out of four. These limitations could not possibly produce a Noah-like caste. The flawed gene/albinism hypothesis, based on a one-time isolated mutation, cannot account for an advanced group of families described as the bluebloods or royals who lived in many regions. A more systemic process is necessary to develop a subspecies consistent with the historical narrative of ABs mixing with early humans.

Nullification: Geneticists believe that humans, unlike animals, have not been around long enough and have not been sufficiently isolated for their genome to have evolved into races or subspecies.[7] Consistent with the AB-IT approach is the fact that science cannot definitively identify a zero-point genetic basis for today's so-called racial categories. Geneticists say identifying the origins for our present phenotype groups is impossible. One reason is that comparisons must be made among the DNA databases of living populations. The samples are geographically incomplete and not "identical to what existed in the past."[8] With the random fractured-gene, accidental-mutation explanation for either albinism or a white, blond, blue-eyed race being disqualified, no other available hypothesis can disprove the Noah narrative. Given our present knowledge of sexual gene-mixing and genetic engineering, the odds that ABs interbred with human females is formidable.

GIANTS

The best-known genotype deviation found in the *Homo sapiens* family tree can be found in the appearance of gigantic skulls and skeletons scattered around the globe. Prior to discovery of the giant fossils now available, the only evidence for giants was in written accounts or artistic images. They were portrayed as nonhuman or half-human. Fortunately, today we can take seriously the stories about ABs and giants. We now have a context based on a time line, a broad sample of fossil measurements, and identified genetic principles. The question is whether we have enough credible data that indicate non-human intervention in humanity's Earthly evolution.

Clues: Chroniclers over millennia have provided clues that ABs had a role in the creation of giants on Earth. For instance, Genesis 6:4 tells us that the sons of ABs (Elohim in this instance) had intercourse with women and produced giants. The biblical books of Amos, Numbers, and others describe a variety of giants: Nephilim, Philistines, Rephaim, and so on. Ancient books from other cultures are generally consistent with these Hebrew sources. Greek reports describe the *gigantes* as warlike and involved with various gods (or ABs, in this context). The early Romans also perpetuated this narrative. One legend has Hercules killing the giant Antaeus. His skeleton was reportedly about 11 feet tall. Such reports have been identified worldwide.

For the last two millennia both scientists and theologians have labeled these historical accounts as myths. To do otherwise would undermine their own professional myths. So today most scholars go along with the idea the ancient-giant idea was made up by naive cavemen types. However, prior to the Current Era, Greek, Egyptian, and Roman historians considered descriptions of giants to be real. They knew that some of the details might be fuzzy, but they did not question the basic authenticity of the events.[9]

Scientists can no longer ignore caches of giant fossils and their origins. However, most try to undermine any hint of alien involvement in history. One such untenable effort is that of Dutch paleontologist Ralph von Koenigswald. He claims (based on a few human-like bone fragments from Java) that all early humans were naturally giants who evolved to a smaller scale.[10] However, anthropologist Martinez has aggregated global evidence that people were once much smaller than modern humans.[11]

Evidence: As of this writing, a dozen well-researched books, including those of Patrick Chouinard,[12] are available on giants. Their reports of huge humanoid fossils demonstrate that the historical reality of giants cannot be questioned. They have met the required tangible-evidence standard. Further analysis is needed, however, to differentiate among various giant types. More research is also needed to sort out time periods, locations, and their relationships with *Homo sapiens*. Scientists have already validated sexual intercourse between humans and Neanderthals. We now need similar DNA comparisons between the fossils of giants and humans from several time-periods and regions to determine who inseminated whom.

Plausibility: We must now assess the plausibility of the three hypotheses. As mentioned previously (Martinez), an evolutionary path from giants to our present generic *Homo sapiens* type is not supported by the fossil record. There is no genetic data record that supports an Earth-based process of gradual evolution. We are left once again with the AB-intervention thesis.

Hundreds of different genes, in more than 180 regions of the body, determine human height.[13] Their specialization and slow rates of mutation are inconsistent with the giants' brief appearance on the stage of human history. To evolve from post-cataclysm humans, averaging 5 feet tall, to 10-foot-tall giants in such a short period requires greater statistical odds than to win the lottery. However,

giant-like ABs having intercourse with human females could produce semi-giants in only one generation. Interestingly enough, the
historical record reports that such a thing actually occurred. After the
period of giants (AB or human, or some admixture thereof) faded
away, the tendency has been toward fewer height differentials among
all human groups and between the sexes.

Nullification: Given the written and image records, the fossil record, and the complex reality of our genome system, the AB-IT explanation for the giants of old stands heads over (pun intended) other
hypotheses. We have no way to prove that it is not true. One version of the AB-IT is that advanced beings could have used genetic-
engineering techniques to develop a species of giants. Whether true
or not, we cannot prove that ABs could not have directly engineered
such earthly giants. However, until physical evidence to the contrary
is validated, the widespread human stories of giants impregnating
normal-sized humans is the winner.

LONGEVITY

It appears that another area of genetically based evidence only
serves to strengthen the AB-IT. It involves the issue of longevity.
Reports from Hebrew, Egyptian,[14] and other ancient cultures claim
early humans lived for several centuries prior to the 11,500 BP cataclysm. In the following millennium they described a point in time
when human lives were suddenly shortened. What appears to be a
foreshortened human internal clock has prevailed for millennia.

Clues: The book of Genesis provides specific names relevant to
this issue. The earliest are seven identified individuals relevant to He-
braic history, from Adam down to Noah, all of whom lived about
900 years. Remember that Noah lived a long time before surviving
the Flood. But after the Flood, the patriarchs' longevity began to
shorten: Shem lived about 600 years, Shelah lived about 400 years,
Terah lived about 200 years, and Abraham and Isaac barely lived past
100. Interestingly, in the book of Genesis an AB quite specifically tells

humans that whatever he did to enable this longevity would no longer apply and that their lives would be reduced to 120 years.[15] Of even of more interest to us is that this length of time is our present biological limit. How could the author have known that we would have a 120-year genetic "off-switch" still in effect the 21st-century human genome?

Evidence: Such significant changes in longevity are not consistent with the rate of evolution of our genes. Again, this points to some kind of external intervention. Obviously we cannot test two fossils of a single person—one as a baby and one as an adult—at the same time; we need another type of evidence. Modern science has given us an excellent test, something called *telomeres*.

Until the late 20th century we had no tools with which to rationalize a discussion about the possible veracity of AB-based longevity in the early periods of human history. Now we know that longevity in humans is controlled by the length of the telomeres in our genes.[16] While we can determine the average length of telomeres at a given age today, we don't have evidence that would differentiate those long-lived humans from us today. While we have some human Y chromosome DNA that is 340,000 years old,[17] no one has reported the condition of its age-related telomeres. What we need are DNA samples from several pre-cataclysm humans and humans between five and 10,000 years ago.

Plausibility: In this case, our evidence is based on alleged conversations between humans and ABs and the annual recording of the extended lives of early humans. At least we now have a science-based foundation to speculate how these ancient narratives could have occurred. If it takes more telomeres to live longer, AB scientists could have figured out how to add to or cut the lengths of telomeres in various species genomes. In this context, we can evaluate Egyptian and Hebrew claims that their ancient leaders lived for hundreds of years, if not thousands. Today's knowledge about genomes and its telomeres is an adequate basis to posit a universal shortening of human telomeres after the Flood. In other words, it is rational to think that ABs could have accomplished the task.

Nullification: The hypothesis that the length of the modern human life span was due to the actions of ABs has a credible physical basis. Further, we can posit that exchanges in which ABs told humans about their actions could be largely correct. While there is some speculation about the details, the most plausible explanation is the AB-IT hypothesis. No current contrary scientific explanation exists that can nullify the AB-IT explanation for the longevity shifts. The AB-IT approach is still the most credible interpretation to date.

CONCLUSIONS

The three areas discussed here are part of a much broader field of research that supports the theory that more advanced beings from elsewhere in the universe have played a significant role in the history of Earth's humans. Some of these areas are the origins of language, alphabets, and writing. The evidence suggests that human institutions have been significantly shaped by the agenda of advanced beings.

The oldest known records of human females producing hybrid progeny involves ABs known as *Neter* ("beings from the skies") in Egyptian accounts. Based on indirect evidence, these activities likely occurred from more than 100,000 years ago until 11,500 BP or later.[18] If we include similar memories passed from generation to generation of Aboriginals in Africa, Oceania, and the Americas, the time frame and scope may be even wider. We don't yet have science available to persuasively pin down the time lines of various *Homo* families. At this point we must depend on a partial fossil record and a speculative model for retroactive DNA dating of mutations or alleged hints of genetic engineering.[19]

After reading this essay, keep in mind that we have only touched fragments of historical accounts of intercourse (sexual and otherwise) between particular ABs and human groups. It is possible that two or more of these accounts may refer to the same event due to different cultures and languages. For instance, the basic narrative of Adam and Eve exists in several cultures, but may date from different periods of this grand DNA swap. The prevailing academic interpretation of so many so-called creation stories is that one very early culture made up a myth that was then disseminated, as early humans scattered about the globe. However, given the presumably narrow scope of imagination in early humanoid species, it is likely that they described actual AB activities rather than concocting myths from nothing.

Fragmented accounts from several cultures, particularly the Sumerians, provide many examples of intervention by more advanced beings with early *Homo sapiens*. Reports of such ABs at this level of intimacy between species are found in many cultures. For instance, Romans believed their tribe's founding father, Romulus, was fathered by Mars with a vestal virgin, a chaste priestess in the temple. This impregnation mixed the blood of an AB and female *Homo sapiens sapiens*.[20] As described previously, a so-called mythical god, Ea, reportedly genetically engineered a hybrid race with more primitive humans.[21]

The ultimate objective of this chapter, based on a few examples, is to leave the reader with a process to present AB-IT evidence and arguments in all forms of public media. Because we cannot directly prove that such events took place, we have used the four steps described in this chapter in order to present a logical evaluation that has more tangible evidence than the skeptics have. The corroborative areas of evidence used in this chapter baffle people like Michael Shermer, founder of the Skeptics Society. They turn to *ad hominem* arguments—appealing to emotions, irrelevant details, or personalities—instead of trying to test the evidence that points to humans as aliens.[22]

~~~

I believe that we are lucky creatures living on a "once-upon-a-time" garden-planet landscape. While we do not yet know when or how our present species first genetically shaped itself, we are inextricably, genetically, and consciously mixed with intelligent beings from other planets and dimensions. We must preserve our home base as long as we can, make peace with extraterrestrial aliens visiting this planet, and simultaneously achieve galactic citizenship for ourselves. Elsewhere, I have attempted a 21st-century understanding of how our self-creative, evolving universe—from a triad of consciousness, subtle energies, and tangible matter—creates the complexity of species among which we humans find ourselves.[23] In this universe, no single species totally dominates its home base or the space that separates all stars and planets. Humans, as the *aliens* we are, can follow more advanced beings with our own potential to become masters of development to boost other civilizations.

Notes

1. Paul Von Ward. *We've Never Been Alone.* Charlottesville, VA: Hampton Roads Publishing, 2011.
2. *Genesis Apocryphon 3.17* of Dead Sea Scrolls (not accepted in the Bible, but clearly of Hebrew origin).
3. D.S Allan and J.B. Delair. *Cataclysm: Compelling Evidence of a Cosmic Catastrophe in 9,500 B.C.* Rochester, Vt.: Bear & Company, 1997.
4. Susan B. Martinez. *Lost History of the Little People.* Rochester, Vt.: Bear & Company, 2013, pp. 156–9.
5. In 1998 the author personally examined some of their mummies in the Nazca Museum in Peru.
6. From *http://realhistoryww.com/world_history/ancient/White_people.htm.*
7. The world's apparent oldest cave art made by Neanderthals adds to the evidence that they were not a distinct species.
8. From *http://harvardmagazine.com/2008/05/race-in-a-genetic-world.html.*

9.   This approach to history is known as *euhemerism*, named for Euhemerus (who practiced it, of course).

10. *Time*. "Science: Giants of Old." October 28, 1946: *http://content.time.com/time/magazine/article/0,9171,804029,00.html#ixzz2jmxfT3GB*.

11. Martinez, *Mysterious Origins of Hybrid Man*.

12. An outstanding array of evidence can be found in Patrick Chouinard's book *Lost Race of the Giants*, published by Bear & Company in 2013.

13. From *www.med.unc.edu/www/newsarchive/2010/september/scientists-stack-up-new-genes-for-height*.

14. The Turin Scroll and Manetho's history indicate that the earliest rulers of Egypt lived for many centuries.

15. Genesis 6:3: "[The AB said] 'My spirit shall not abide in man for ever, for that he also is flesh; therefore shall his days be a hundred and twenty years.'"

16. *Telomeres* are caps of repetitive DNA at the end of our chromosomes. We have 10,000 at birth, but our regular cell divisions may reduce them to 5,000. With optimum health they will last us 120 years.

17. From *www.newscientist.com/article/dn23240-the-father-of-all-men-is-340000-years-old.html#*.

18. Von Ward, *We've Never Been Alone*.

19. David A. Plaiste. "Mitochondrial DNA Mutation Rates": *www.cs.unc.edu/~plaisted/ce/mitochondria.html*.

20. This practice is the origin of blue-blooded royals who became the rulers of various tribes or city-states.

21. Wespenre.com: "Anunnaki Paper #2: Genesis or the 'Genes of Isis'?" *www.wespenre.com/genes-of-isis.htm*.

22. From *www.skeptic.com*.

23. Paul Von Ward. *Children of a Learning Universe*. Charlottesville, Va.: Hampton Roads Publishing, 2014.

A Tale of Three Continents: Homer's Epics and the Real War on Troy

By Steven Sora

The written record of the Trojan War has been around for about 2,700 years. Transmitted through his poetry, Homer tells the story in two major parts: The *Iliad* is the tale of the last few weeks of a long war, with the vengeful Acheans (Greeks) taking their siege machine to a place called Ilium (Troy), where they battle for 10 years, only to achieve victory by trickery. The second part is the *Odyssey*, the tale of Ulysses trying to return to his homeland while suffering the wrath of the gods. His misadventures bring him around the world for another nine years, before the final challenge he faces upon reaching home. The epics, taken together, present a great story, a masterpiece of literature unrivaled in its time. The problem is that although the story may be based on reality, it is seriously flawed as a historical record. Homer, born in Turkey near the place where he said Troy existed, moved to the island of Chios, where he achieved his fame. His story, however, was pieced together from a war fought in a place quite distant from Turkey, in the area where Plato placed Atlantis, in fact. As we shall see, the real Troy lies on the Atlantic coast, where statues of the gods poke out of the sands of coastal Portugal.

The Ancient Search for a Lost City

The greatest problem with the *Iliad* is that there were no Greeks in Greece circa 1200 BC, which is when the story was supposed to have taken place. In the texts, Achaeans, Argives, and Danaans are mentioned, but neither the adjective nor the noun *Greek* is ever

117

mentioned until later translations. Moreover, there were never a people called Trojans in the modern area of Turkey where Troy was supposed to have existed. The Hittites, who actually controlled Anatolia, as Turkey was once called, were meticulous record-keepers. They kept lists of goods bought, sold, traded, and shipped from city to city, records of kings and princes, and a compilation of their own histories. And yet there are no records of Trojans and certainly no Troy. Neither is there any mention of Trojans among any ancient Egyptian writings.

Not only was there no Greek nation at that time, but there were no great, epic victories achieved by peoples of the area that became Greece. In fact, the nation that is now Greece seemed to be the on the losing side of some kind of disaster that occurred circa 1200 BC. More than three quarters of the cities and towns that existed in 1200 BC were gone by 1100 BC, evidence of a dark age precipitated by some kind of natural disaster, such as a great flood, or a successful raid from the sea.

The evidence for treating Homer's tale as history is even more disappointing. Homer's Troy was a great, sprawling city defended by mighty walls and towers. Scholars envisioned that it held 50,000 people. Homer tells us that 50 princes had their palaces within the city. He describes wide streets and broad avenues, with temples to Athena and Apollo. The Turkish site commonly agreed upon in modern times, however, seems barely large enough to hold 5,000 people—about the size of an average shopping center.

Records of the search for Troy start 150 years after Homer's tale was penned circa 775 BC. The results were disappointing across the board. Alexander the Great marched to where he thought Troy had existed, in Anatolia/Turkey, only to find no Troy (or Ilion or Ilium, other names for the city). Because there was no temple of Athena, Alexander had one built; he installed a cult of Athena where he felt there should have been one. Because there was no city he had one built, as well. He sacrificed to the once-mighty king Priam and claimed that the single column that still stood must have been erected to Achilles. Despite Alexander's insistence that Troy was in Anatolia/Turkey, his own court geographer, Eratosthenes, was of the notion that the *Odyssey* took place outside the gates of Hercules—that is, in the Atlantic Ocean. He believed that Troy could not have been where his king claimed it was, but he kept that opinion to himself.

Julius Caesar was the next man of fame to visit the Ilium of Alexander. The Romans were fond of claiming they descended from Troy or Greece, but Caesar, who believed he was from the family of Ilus (Ilium), was disappointed by what he found. Even the buildings erected as Alexander's Troy were in ruins. However, that did not stop Virgil from linking Rome to a defeat of Troy in his epic, *The Aeneid*. Constantine wanted to make the Ilium of Alexander his capital, too, but he chose not to as there was no seaport.

After reading of a 10-year siege by sea in this epic, one wonders why such early historians did not notice that Ilium was actually inland. It may have been that the venerable writers Herodotus, Xenophon, Arrian, and Plutarch simply held Alexander in near-god status: How could he be wrong about the location of Troy? However, Plutarch agreed with Eratosthenes that the book that followed *The Iliad*, *The Odyssey*, started and ended somewhere in the Atlantic.

The Modern Search for Troy

In more modern times several different locales near the Ilium "discovered" by Alexander were suggested as possible sites of the real Troy. In 1785 two Frenchmen, Jean-Baptiste Lechevalier and Count Choiseul Gouffier, proposed a site at Balli Dag because there was a hot spring there, as described in Homer. In 1822, five miles from Balli Dag, Turkey, another place, called Hisarlik, was claimed by Charles McLaren, an editor of the *Encyclopedia Brittanica*. At the time he had not visited the site but simply reviewed topographical maps in order to come up with his theory.

The Golden Age of archeology was dawning. It actually was not "golden" by modern standards, as it was essentially a destructive attack on priceless sites all around the world. Tombs were looted, artifacts stolen or destroyed, and theft was even institutionalized, as one nation literally stole another's history. Into this new dubious era, along came Heinrich Schliemann. One biographer, David A. Traill, describes him as a pathological liar, a destroyer of evidence who falsified excavation reports and who purchased his treasures to salt the sites he "discovered." Schliemann even went as far as claiming that he had discovered a Trojan coin. The coin in question, however, was a coin he had bought and that was minted by Emperor Commodus circa 180–192 AD. The Greeks claimed he had looted many objects from their country, and Schliemann himself admitted to taking no fewer than 8,700 golden objects from the treasury of Priam. While there are many flaws in Schliemann's claims, he was the toast of Europe for years. At the same time he became disillusioned: "Nothing was as he envisioned, no palace on the summit, no Bronze Age tools of which Homer had sung" (from *Finding the Walls of Troy* by Susan Allen).

By the year 2000 there were at least 25 excavations in the area of Troy. Yet, there were no examples of Bronze Age writing, no cuneiform, and no Linear B tablets to be found in the area near Troy, nor any other place in the western Mediterranean that could have been Troy. The site of Troy, so painstakingly excavated, shows no evidence of a siege, either. The lack of any real evidence in both the ancient story and the modern discoveries was an embarrassment to serious historians. To attract tourism, walls were built, sites were named, and the Trojan Horse, if one ever existed, was re-created in modern times to give the "city" an amusement-park look. Even *The Cambridge Ancient History* (Volume II) weighs in by pointing out that of the 170 places named with Homer's texts, only 80 have every been found, and of them, only half existed in Mykenaean times. Most of the names given for the Pylos area of modern Greece are not even tentatively traceable. The place from which Odysseus emerged has no Mykenaean remains.

Most remarkably, the inland area of the Bosphorus contains no pounding surf or loud waves, as mentioned by Homer. The blind poet seemed to set his story in an oceanic context, with repeated mentions of waves and tides and a "loud sounding sea." Homer used the word *okeanos* to describe the Mediterranean Sea, though no other writer made that connection. Instead all others described the "river" outside the Mediterranean that surrounded their world, as the ocean. As well, Homer describes hot and cold springs where the Trojan women would launder their clothing, but only one has been found, several days' walk from Hisarlik, which, as we now know, is where Schliemann placed Troy.

There are other dead-ends. The vegetation of Homer includes the beech tree, willows, and black poplar, all of which are more likely to be found in a north-Atlantic climate than in the warmer Mediterranean areas. Another historical inaccuracy is that the Achaeans ride into battle on chariots made just for transportation, whereas the Hittites of the Anatolian plane fought the Egyptians around the same time but never got out of their chariots. And finally, the distance from where the Greeks might have sailed to the place that might have been Troy was actually only a five-day sail in the type of ships in use circa 1200 BC, ships that employed both sail and oar. Why, then, would they have to stay away from home for a decade during the foreign war?

If not in Turkey...

Circa 1200 BC, the time period that both ancient and modern historians give as the rough time frame of the Trojan War, events in the Atlantic took place that led to disastrous results in the Mediterranean Sea. First, there was a war in which leagues of cities fought each other for trade supremacy. The war was followed by an even greater calamity that displaced possibly hundreds of thousands of people. These displaced people became known as the sea peoples, and the histories of their various nations record their invasion of the Mediterranean Sea. Many enjoyed the refuge of the inner sea, the

Mare Nostrum ("our sea"), as the Greeks called it, and stayed. Some of these groups even reached Egypt, which only survived by hiring them as mercenaries, essentially buying them off. The Shardan (alternately the Sherdan or Shardana) peoples may have ranged throughout the entire Mediterranean, but settled on Sardinia. They have been described as being very much like the Danes of what later became Denmark, in terms of their warrior dress. Egypt, once again having no mention of Trojans, does mention the sea-going Shardan. Egyptian records claim that they were defeated and sent back to settle Sardinia. Historian Michael Wood believes they were the first of the raiders circa 1200 BC to enter the Mediterranean and disrupt trade.

The term *Pelasgians* may have been used to collectively describe all of the sea peoples; the term *Peleset* describes a particular group of people who settled the eastern coast of the Mediterranean, where they became known as the Philistine or Palestine peoples. The Semitic root P-L-SH means "to wander" or "to invade." Just as the Vikings of the Atlantic did, the Peleset did both. They settled numerous cities, including Ashdod, Askelon, Gath, and Gaza. The king of Gath was Achish, which bears more than passing similarity to the name of the Trojan prince Anchises. A third discrete group was known as the Lukka. They, too, sailed into the Mediterranean and settled in Anatolia. The same Hittite texts that somehow missed the Trojans recorded the Lukka.

The Sikels were another tribe that reached and settled Sicily at this time, circa 1200 BC. Their historical records are sparse, as Sicily was settled by numerous invasions over the years, including the Greeks 600 years later. It is not even certain if their language was in the Indo-European family.

Possibly one of the most important groups was the Tyrsenoi, or the Teresh peoples. The vowel-less Egyptians described them as the *Trs*. The Romans called them the Etrusci, Tusci (as in Tuscany), and Thusci. Herodotus claims they are the Etruscans. The Etruscans pre-dated the Roman civilization but were deliberately discredited to claim all innovation started with Rome. However, it was the Etruscans who planned cities on a grid, and built the walls, tunnels, aqueducts, and roadways that existed in Roman times. Their word for the courtyards they included in their homes was *atria* (*atrium* in the singular). Their word for harbor was *hatrium*, and they had a city on the mouth of the Po, called Adria, which then gave the Adriatic Sea its name.

While Rome tried to summarily delete the Etruscans from their history, literature kept them alive. In Italy Virgil tells us that the Etruscan people revived an unusual game that they used to enact many years before. It was the "game of Troy," a complicated military rite incorporating armed dancers and horseback riders who traverse a labyrinth. One surviving Etruscan vase shows the word *Truia* outside the labyrinth. This game or ritual was also celebrated in Scandinavia, England, and France. In England, *Caer Droia* survives in the Welsh language as the "fort of Troy." There are many locales that feature labyrinths in France, perhaps the most important of which is the Basilica of Notre Dame, in St. Omer. Alternately called Troy Towns, these labyrinths can be found today in Italy and Crete, and as far east as Egypt.

There is other evidence from areas in the Atlantic that serves to place both stories in a pre-Celtic world, a world that employed a pre-Celtic language that survives as Breton, Welsh, and Old Irish. The Celtic word *Tro* means "a place of turning." A game, a ritual, or possibly a game evolved from a ritual, it may have lost its significance over the years. It may have evolved as the real events of 1200 BC were remembered as real. Some cataclysmic event, such as war or natural disaster—or both—took place. It was large enough to disrupt all of the peoples that lived outside of the Pillars of Hercules and send then eastward into the Mediterranean Sea for safety. This was no ordinary earthquake, however. The evidence points to something much larger. Regardless, the evidence sea peoples that moved into the Mediterranean and upset the order of things is clear and substantial. There is evidence that a massive movement of population took place all around the Atlantic, as well.

ENGLAND'S TROY

Geoffrey of Monmouth, writing in the 12th century, built onto the histories of other important writers of the isles, several whom he had used as sources. He starts with the story of Aeneas, who flees Troy and lands in Italy. The story of Britain starts with a massive migration from Troy through France and out to the Atlantic. He tells of a final battle between the Trojan-Britons and the Greeks, in which the Greeks are defeated. He traces the descendants to the exile Brutus, who reorganized groups of Trojans from the war and brought them to England after sacrificing to the goddess Diana, who, through an augur, predicted that "a race of kings will be born there from your stock and the round circle of the whole earth will be subject to them" (from Geoffrey, *The History of the Kings of Britain*). The Trojan fleet, under Brutus, sailed to Britain, alternatively known as Alba, where Brutus founds Troia Nova, the New Troy on the River Thames. Geoffrey further explains that in that "race of kings" was a man named Lud who inherited the city of New Troy and built great walls and gates around it. The gate named for this king, Ludgate, would over the years give its name to the entire city: London.

Geoffrey's story was accepted as history until the 18th century, when the Hanoverian Germans tried to erase everything British, going as far as outlawing the Welsh language. Yet, Edward I, who had conquered Wales, wanted it named Troylebaston. Queen Elizabeth I was once greeted as "that sweet remain of Priam's state, that hope of springing Troy." All of this was accepted as history; Chaucer, Milton, William of Malmesbury, and even Shakespeare mention the Trojan's founding. Yet later in Shakespeare's *Henry V*, a character is twice described as a "base Trojan."

France and the Family of King Priam

In France, seventh-century historian Fredegar spent 35 years chronicling the history of his people. France was not yet a country at that time, but rather a handful of provinces and kingdoms ruled by the Sicambrians of the Franks. Fredegar's history is remarkable in that for such an early work, it cited numerous sources. Fredegar said it was King Priam of the Trojans who was the oldest ancestor. His story is not without merit.

Other historians have written on the origin of the name Paris, the city of the Parisi people, named for Paris of the *Iliad*. The center of Paris was once a shrine to the goddess of light, Lutetia. She is situated on the Seine River, named for the moon goddess Sin. Paris itself is not far from Troyes, a French city of learning from at least medieval times. It was here that St. Bernard chose to charter the Knights Templar, and here that the Grail literature came into being. This New Troy, as it might have been called, was said to have been the place that 12,000 Trojans, refugees from the war, settled. In Normandy lies Trouville-sur-Mer, literally "Troy town by the sea." Other Trojan-like names include Tournai and Troarn. Tournai was home to a great treasure find that uncovered 300 golden bees, a golden Apis bull, and a statue of Isis.

Then there is the city of Ypres. This is the city of Priam (legend here in horthern France has Priam bringing his people to safety). Remarkably the legend has survived numerous centuries up until today. In both France and England, modern De la Priem, Pryme, and Prime families share not only such a long-held belief, but a family motto: *Nil Invita Minerva*, meaning "nothing contrary to Minerva." As the post-Homeric works have exiles of Troy passing through Italy, France, and England, this motto may have been picked up along the way.

SCANDINAVIA'S ULYSSES?

Trondheim was once the capital of Norway, and it was already old when Christianity came into the region. Similar to the name Troy, the place-names of Trondheim, Troja, and Troai all begin with Celtic root word *Tro*. In much of Scandinavia, Christianity did its best to stamp out pagan roots, although some cathedrals still have standing stones, megalithic clues to a much older religion in the distant past, near their walls. Trondheim's Church of Saint Mary was built over an eighth-century temple to Freyja, the bride of the Norse god Thor.

One of Homer's greatest heroes was Ulysses (Ull or Ullr, as he was known in Scandinavia from ancient times). Part god, part hero, he was the son of a goddess, Sif, who lost her husband soon after Ulysses was born. He may be the first "son of a widow," a common motif for the Templar Knights and modern Freemasons. He is mentioned in several works that survive from most ancient times. The tale of the war between the Aesar and the Vanna may actually describe events that occurred sometime after 2000 BC, when the climate grew sharply colder and the people of the Steppes (Asians) moved into the territory of the Vanna (Northern Europe). The Vanna people already lived in the isles and places that might have given memorial to Ullr, including Ullapool in Scotland, Ullswater in England, and Ulster in Ireland. Ullr is remembered in numerous Norse locations, as well: Uleraker is "Ullr's field," Ullevi is "Ull's sanctuary," Ullarhvall is "Ullr's hill."

Ull was chosen to lead after Odin was pushed out of his role for various crimes he committed. In Lilia Ullevi, Sweden, a shrine to Ullr was recently unearthed. When the shrine was discovered 65 rings were also unearthed on which it is believed oaths are engraved. These so-called Rings of Ullr are actually mentioned in the Atlakviöa, an Eddic poem. Author Felice Vinci places the travels of Ulysses in the Baltic and Northern seas of Scandinavia, and believes that Ullr and Ulysses, the archer and the warrior, are one and the same.

Discovering the Real Troy

The real Trojan War was fought on the coast of the Atlantic Ocean, perhaps ranging as far south as the North African coast and as far north as Scandinavia. The real Troy was part of a much larger Atlantean kingdom in which three centralized cities ruled the sea. Moving from north to south, the first of these was Lisbon. Its name after the collapse of Troy was Alis Ubbo, meaning the "port of Ulysses." It underwent changes in spelling over the years, and its geography was shaped by catastrophe. It once had the hot springs where Homer's women washed their clothing. Just south of Lisbon is the second city, Setubal, a name possibly more ancient than Lisbon describing a god rather than a mere hero. A Celtic-based word, *Setu* is reminiscent of the Latin *in situ*, combined with a god-name revered from Ireland and Scandinavia to the eastern end of the Mediterranean, known as Bal or Baal. It is the fourth-largest town in modern Spain. And further south is the third city, still on the map today, and still named Troia. Together these three cities were home to the Atlantean sea god Poseidon, and thus may have been represented by the Trident.

Driving south from Lisbon for research that culminated in my book *Triumph of the Sea Gods*, it was startling to notice how the land simply drops off into the sea; a tall headland quickly becomes a flat beach at sea level. This is the result of more than one catastrophic event—a hurricane out at sea, a tsunami hitting land, and a coastal people destroyed. The first time the area was struck by such a calamity, the Romans named the surviving town Cetobriga. *Ceto* is the root word that gives us the word *whale*; in Roman times it meant "sea monster." Perhaps this whale or sea monster was the beast Scylla that threatened Ulysses. Troy today lies between two rivers, the Tejo and the Sado. At the mouth of the Sado is Torre de Outao, where a temple to Neptune greets incoming ships. Statues of the Atlantean heroes and gods at times poke out of the sands.

So it is very possible that this long-fought war at sea was then followed by a major catastrophe. Plato, writing circa 350 BC, actually describes something very similar in his tale of Atlantis. A great war is fought between the Athenians, who did not exist in Plato's controversial time frame of 9000 BC (controversial because many believe the extreme date must have been in lunar months, not solar years), and the Atlanteans. At the end of the war, a massive earthquake and tsunami destroy the entire Atlantean kingdom. The island disappears "in a day and a night." This coincides with the time frame of Immanuel Velikovsky, who, in his *Worlds in Collision*, claims a great upheaval threatened the earth starting in less controversial date of 1600 BC.

To understand what happened to the cities of the trident—Lisbon, Setubal, and Troia—in 1200 BC, one need only look to what happened there in more modern times. On November 1, 1755, All Saints Day as celebrated in Catholic Portugal, a massive earthquake hit Lisbon. Approximately 60,000 people perished in what is estimated to have been an 8.9 or even a 9-plus on the Richter scale. Only two earthquakes are known to have been greater. The oceanic lithosphere, the hard shell of the earth, simply collapsed somewhere out to sea. Three tsunamis followed in rapid order and yet the worst was not over. Fires broke out in churches where candles burned and in homes where cooking was unattended by churchgoers. The fires would rage for an entire week.

The effects were not limited to Lisbon, but were felt as far south as Morocco, where they caused damage to coastal cities and even inland. An estimated 60,000 additional lives were lost in this country alone. Tsunamis also hit Ireland and France and even the West Indies, where water levels rose three feet. Thought lightning may not strike twice, apparently massive earthquakes do. Troia/Cetobriga recorded another such disaster in 412 AD. Could an even earlier catastrophe have served as the catalyst to a post-war massive migration?

The Hometown of Ulysses?

The modern city of Cadiz lies just outside the gates of Hercules, today called the Straits of Gibraltar. Cadiz is an important port on the Atlantic coast of Spain; evidence suggests that it was settled as long ago as 3000 BC. Cadiz was once two islands, one of which was named Leon. This separate island, as Ilion, means "the isle of Leon." According to Adolf Schulten, a German archeologist, this entire area was once a "golden triangle," a higher civilization, in the distant past. The three points of the triangle were Huelva on the coast further north, Cadiz to the south, and Seville, an inland city with access to the coast during that period, to the northeast. According to mythology Seville was the creation of Hercules and Atlas. A massive temple to Hercules and a labyrinth existed there well before the Iliad was committed to writing. So did temples to Astarte and Baal, although these are now submerged.

Phoenicians would visit and then settle Seville and other Iberian cities, and impose their own god, Melkarth, over Hercules. Long before Hercules and Melkarth, Cadiz was named for Eumolpus, one of the children of Poseidon. The city was protected then, as now, by a fortress that extended into the sea over a long causeway, complete with three switchbacks. The fortress is today known as San Sebastian, named for a saint with mythological roots who replaced Chronos, the god who once ruled. When the Phoenicians arrived they called the city Gades, or Gadir, meaning "fortified place."

Establishing the case for Cadiz and the trident cities further north being locked in the epicenter of a war fits the description of a place that regularly heard the pounding surf and crashing waves, which Homer place inland near the Bosporus. Here wind and fog are more common than seas of blue that occur in the land where Homer penned his works. Indeed, while Schliemann would claim Ithaka in Greece was the home of Ulysses, no palace was found there, only six shards and a wall. And anyway, the city was named long after Homer's life ended.

Tales of the Brave Ulysses

There are certain major differences between the two epics. The *Odyssey* can be described as a Celtic tale, or *immram*. The people who lived in the Atlantic coastal communities and islands may more correctly be described as pre-Celtic, but we know little about people and civilizations that existed pre-1200 BC. The Celts may have carried on and expanded a more ancient culture, just as the Romans superimposed themselves over the Etruscan population and inherited their achievements. The Celtic immran always involves travel, usually to islands. It also takes on a supernatural air, with spirits and gods and the like.

Odysseus the warrior is described by Homer as a "sacker of cities." He is also described as the son of Laertes, which may have been just a name to Homer's audience, but in Breton and Welsh, the preserved language of a Celtic world, a *laer* is a thief. Was Ulysses taking advantage of the post-war collapse of the world order, just to bring home some booty like a common pirate? Homer has him reaching Ismarus (the stronghold of the Cicones, located in present-day Greece). Ulysses is successful in sacking the city but lingers too long: When he and his 108 men set out to sea they run into a storm that pushes them even farther out. Celtic tales recall the place-names: *Is-Maris* (meaning "isles of the sea") and *Caer Iz*, possibly once a real city that met the fate of drowning in a Celtic tale. (Interestingly, tales of flooded and underwater villages and cities occur from France all the way to the Baltic.) Ulysses and his men are blown out to sea in a straight line for more than nine days. This is impossible in the Mediterranean Sea, but very possible in the Atlantic Ocean. When the storm dies down, Ulysses and his men find themselves in the land of the Lotus Eaters. There may never be any way of saying with certainty, but this could be Jerba in the Mediterranean, it could be Senegal (according to Iman Wilkens), or it could be closer to the straits of Gibraltar, the Cape Verde Islands. Africa's Cape Verde Islands were once called the Gorgonides, the children of the Gorgon, which probably dates them to ancient times. The Canary Islands are yet another contender. When the Spanish reached this group of islands in more modern times, they met a people who had once sailed there but lost the art of sailing. Possibly they were descendants of a displaced peoples post-1200 BC.

Next, Ulysses/Odysseus comes to the famous land of the Cyclops. When the giant sleeps, Ulysses puts a sharp stick through his one eye. His fellow giants hear him scream and yell to him, asking: "Who is hurting you?" The Cyclops declares, "Noman is hurting me." The actual word used in the Odyssey for *Noman* was *Outis*; in Celtic this means "sharp stick." While Homer might have missed the point in recording this story, Celtic bards were artists of punning.

Next comes the "island of the winds," Aeolia, ruled by the king Aeolus. By this time misadventures have reduced Ulysses's fleet to one ship. The single surviving ship of Ulysses is blown across an ocean for days. Again, this is problematic if we are talking about the Mediterranean Sea, as one would eventually find landfall much sooner than that. When Ulysses reaches the island the king gives him a bag to tie to his ship, with the caveat that he should not open it. The curious men aboard Ulysses's ship give in to curiosity and open the bag. The bag contains winds that blow them back to Aeolia. The king then believes the stars are against Ulysses and sends him and his men away.

Taken at face value, this part of the story makes little sense. It takes on greater meaning when we understand that the Celtic word *bag* meant "boat." In this context, the king may have repaired their ship or even replaced it. (Incidentally, the letter A, as found here in the king's name and that of the island, has always been associated with water. In the Sumerian language the word for the sea was simply *A*. In Old Norse it was *Aa*, and in the Scottish-Gaelic it was *Ae*. The pre-Celtic term *Al* implied flowing water.)

Next Ulysses runs into the Laestrygonian cannibals, an encounter with no directional clue in Homer's *Odyssey*. (Directional clues have been used by other writers who make claims regarding the "map" of Ulysses's travels. The location of the Laestrygonian cannibals frustrates all such attempts.) After this encounter Ulysses is probably as far north as he ever ventures in his travels. He comes to an island where Circe rules. She may have been a much more powerful goddess than the story allows. She is the source of the sacred Circle, the sanctuary that keeps evil out. Her circle, or *cirkle,* in a Christianized world becomes *kirkos,* and in the Orkney Islands north of Scotland, the Kirk. In the largest populated area in those islands is the city of Kirkwall, where the Cathedral of St. Magnus dominates the town.

After a year of living well, Ulysses and his men tire of what was, for all intents and purposes, their captivity. Before they leave, Circe has one chore for them to complete, a visit to Hades. They fear no one before them has ever reached Hades and returned. They eventually reach Hades and receive news of the living from the dead. Achilles, who once enjoyed glory as a warrior, now wishes he could live even as a slave rather than be a dead king of the dead. He is a talking head now, like the Irish Bran or the Templars' Baphomet. Ulysses survives his visit to Hades, and visits Circe one last time to get directions home.

There is no smooth sailing, however, as they pass among the sirens, whose singing lures men to their deaths. Again we are more likely to be in the Orkneys, where hundreds of sea-pigs appear as that many heads above the water. Those who sail in the Orkneys are often shocked to see what resembles drowning people but are simply seals. Thousands of seabirds, kittiwakes, and guillemots screech overhead, and the howling winds make these icy waters seem like a hellish place. Their siren-like cries might be compared to those same Sirens who haunted Ulysses.

Scylla and Charybdis are next. The legend of Scylla was old long before Homer. She was a moon goddess who cut off the sun king's hair to steal his power. Her myth remained as the Delilah of the Bible who stole Samson's strength by cutting off his hair. This next adventure of Ulysses and his crew had the hero and his men between a whirlpool and a monster. Again, an Orkney Islands setting may be more appropriate here. The isle of Stroma today has two whirlpools and a massive seal colony. In the ancient tongue it was *Seil-aa*, or "seal waters."

Finally Ulysses picks up a fortunate fair wind that blows his ship to the south. He reaches a triangular island where Helios grazes his cattle. As Ulysses sleeps, his men steal and roast the cattle. As they leave the island a black cloud and huge storm wreck their ship. Only Ulysses survives. Pre-Celtic survival words give off clues where this island may have been. The Breton word *heol* means "sun." It survives at Stonehenge as the misnamed heelstone. The Welsh language has a word *Ap-Heol*, or "son of the sun." This word gives us the name of the god Apollo, or Ap-Ul in Egypt. He was the opener of the ways. According to the Greek explorer Pytheas, Apollo visited Stonehenge every 19 years, giving us a clue that the story served more than one purpose. A 19-year cycle, today called the *metonic cycle*, describes the amount of time needed for the lunar and solar calendars to reconcile. This may indicate that the Odyssey was at once a hero's tale *and* a lesson about the procession of the sun and moon.

After drifting for nine days, Ulysses lands on Calypso. The eponymous sea nymph is at the same time terrible and beautiful. As Kali, she was once an all-powerful goddess who was worshipped from India to Ireland. In Ireland, her priestesses were known as *kelle*. They were star watchers who recorded the days, giving us the word calendar. Again, this adds to the case for a hidden knowledge being transmitted. But by whom? The poet Homer, or those who transmitted the story from the Atlantic to the Mediterranean. All of these details are important in making the case that the references in Homer, his literary and historical antecedents, were much, much older than Homer was at the time he wrote these texts. As well, they underline my point that the original deities (like Circe) were often female, and that Homer's rewrite reduced them to one-dimensional characters, although still powerful ones.

Ulysses petitions the gods to leave and, finally, reaches home in Ithaka. Here he battles the 108 suitors of his wife Penelope with his arrows and emerges victorious. Ulysses starts his quest with 108 men, and now kills 108 men, thus providing a sense of balance and closure for the reader. Interestingly, the number 108 is sacred in many traditions; for example, there are 108 *stupas* in Angkor Wat and 108 halls in Valhalla. Perhaps this is yet another example of the ancient literary antecedents that Homer was drawing on in his narratives.

Homer's Phoenician Inspiration

The Phoenicians were known to have used Atlantic ports at least as early as 1200 BC. These seafarers are credited for bringing the love of all things purple as well as the red wines of Spain, which the Cretans called *foinos*. They may have also be one of the earliest peoples to reach Ireland. The beloved Fenian Cycle of Irish folkore tells of a people who crossed from Iberia to the land of Hibernia. In the lands of the pre-Celtic bards, writing took a backseat to being able to recite such tales. Finn Mac Cool, the greatest Fenian hero, attempts to get his wife back from an interloper; in order to do so, like Ulysses, he must go into the underworld. Bards could recite such cycles from memory.

Possibly the greatest gift brought to the modern world by the Phoenicians, however, was the alphabet. They had started using their 22-letter alphabet around 1200 BC, and brought it to the Mediterranean world sometime around 800 BC. Our word "phonetics," of course, establishes the source of writing using letters. The Greeks became not only the beneficiaries of the means to write, but they also received the tales of a great war and a widely traveled hero from the Phoenicians, peoples who had actually originated in the Atlantic. Homer had merely converted these newly imported tales into a narrative and a style that his audience understood.

In essence, Homer took a much older story of a major war fought 500 years before he was born, and then recast that story for modern Greek sensibilities. At the same time he deceived historians for thousands of years by placing his Troy in Asia. The name "Troy" has survived the ravages of time, weather, and disasters (both natural and man-made), and remains on the map today as Troia.

BIBLIOGRAPHY

Allen, Susan Hueck. *Finding the Walls of Troy.* Los Angeles, Calif.: University of California, 1999.

Baring, Ann, and Jules Cashford. *The Myth of the Goddess.* New York: Arkana/Penguin, 1991.

Begg, Ean. *The Cult of the Black Virgin.* London: Arkana 1996.

Blegen, Carl W. *Troy and the Trojans.* New York: Frederick A. Praeger, 1963.

Bloch, Raymond. *The Etruscans.* New York: Cowles Books, 1969.

Bonwich, James. *Irish Druids and Old Irish Religions.* New York: Barnes & Noble, 1986 (originally published in 1894).

Bradford, Ernle. *Ulysses Found.* New York: Harcourt and Brace & World, 1963.

Condos, Theony. *Star Myths of the Greeks and Romans.* Grand Rapids, Mich.: Phanes Press 1997

Conrad, Jack Randolph. *The Horn and the Sword.* New York: EP Dutton and Co., 1957.

De Boer, Jelle Zeilinga, and Donald Theodore Sanders. *Earthquakes in Human History.* Princeton, N.J.: Princeton University Press, 2003.

Dothan, Trude, and Moshe Dothan. *People of the Sea, The Search for the Philistines.* New York: MacMillan Publishing, 1992.

Drews, Robert. *The End of the Bronze Age.* Princeton, N.J.: Princeton University Press, 1993.

Flemming, Nicholas C. *Cities in the Sea.* Garden City, N.Y.: Doubleday, 1971.

Geoffrey of Monmouth (Thorpe Lewis trans.). *The History of the Kings of Britain.* Middlesex, UK: Penguin, 1966.

Homer. *The Iliad.* Translated by Martin Hammond. London: Penguin Classics, 1987.

Homer. *The Odyssey.* Translated by W.H. Rouse. New York: Penguin, 1937.

James, Simon. *The Atlantic Celts.* Madison: University of Wisconsin Press, 1999.

Julius Caesar. *The Conquest of Gaul.* (S.A. Hanford, trans.) London: Penguin, 1951.

Latacz, Joachim. *Troy and Homer, Towards a Solution of an Old Mystery.* New York: Oxford University Press, 2004.

MacCulloch, J.A. *The Religion of the Ancient Celts.* London: Studio Editions, 1992 (reprinted from 1911 edition).

Markale, Jean. *Women of the Celts.* Rochester, Vt.: Inner Traditions, 1986.

MacKendrick, Paul. *The Iberian Stones Speak.* New York: Funk & Wagnalls, 1969.

McCaffrey, Carmel and Leo Eaton. *In Search of Ancient Ireland.* Chicago, Ill.: New Amsterdam Books, 2002.

McClusky, Stephen C. *Astronomies and Cultures in Early Medieval Europe.* New York: Cambridge University Press, 1998.

Savory, H.N. *Spain and Portugal.* New York: Frederick A. Praeger, 1968.

Schlain, Leonard. *The Alphabet and the Goddess.* New York: Penguin/ Arkana, 1998.

Severin, Tim. *The Ulysses Voyage, Sea Search for the Odyssey.* London: Hutchinson Ltd., 1987.

Traill, David A. *Schliemann of Troy, Treasure and Deceit.* New York: St. Martin's Press, 1995.

Verlikovsky, Immanuel. *Peoples of the Sea.* New York: Doubleday, 1977.

Walker, Barbara. *The Woman's Encyclopedia of Myths and Secrets.* San Francisco, Calif.: Harper & Row, 1983.

West, John Anthony. *Serpent in the Sky.* Wheaton, Ill.: Theosophical Publishing House, 1993.

Whitshaw, Elena Maria. *Atlantis in Spain.* Stelle, Ill.: AUP, 2002.

Wilkens, Iman. *Where Troy Once Stood.* New York: St. Martin's Press, 1991.

Wood, Michael. *In Search of the Trojan War.* New York: New American Library, 1985.

A Starry Drama: Astroceremonial Architecture and Humanity's Path to the Heavens

By Thomas Brophy

Polestars and Precession

Bedouin nomads have always used the constant polestar and its starry companions to navigate when traveling vast distances through the desert at night. Today Polaris is our polestar, but that was not always so. Earth is tilted so every year the Sun migrates familiarly north and south between the tropic lines. By a similar but less familiar and much longer-term motion, the Earth's tilted spin axis wobbles its direction around a circle in the sky every 26,000 years and the "fixed" stars migrate up and down in declination. And as Earth's axis wobbles, it points through a slowly drifting set of polestars. The star closest to the pole is what we call the polestar. About 14,000 years ago it was a very different star—the brilliant Vega in the Grecian Lyra constellation, brightest star in all the north. My calculations show that for a brief span of years, a few human lifetimes, at a special time in Vega's precession cycle, and a very special human time the ancient Egyptians called Zep Tepi, the origin time of humanity, this mother of all polestars shined down an extremely precisely hewn long passage extending underneath what is now known as the Great Pyramid of Khufu at Giza. At least, Vega would have if the shaft had been there at the time. And there is gradually mounting evidence that just maybe it *was* there. But we are getting ahead of ourselves; first we must touch on the astroceremonial symbolic architecture of much more recent times.

MEGALITHS AND STARS

In the book I coauthored with Robert Bauval, *Black Genesis: The Prehistoric Origins of Ancient Egypt*, we discuss an intriguing connection between the astroceremonial culture of the prehistoric peoples of Nabta Playa, and the symbology in the monumental architecture of the earliest temples of the Nile Valley civilization—the people who built the Great Pyramids. We show how the megalithic stone alignments of Nabta emphasize the stars of the circumpolar region—the stars that rotate nightly around the north star. The people of Nabta Playa and their successors, the Nile Valley temple building civilization, tracked the circumpolar stars of the Big Dipper (called the Bull's Thigh by the ancient Egyptians) together with the annual rising of Sirius and the stars of Orion's Belt. In this essay I look even further back in time to evidence for tracking of a different north star at a much earlier time.

First, I review the astroceremonialism of Nabta Play before 5000 BCE. In *Black Genesis* and *Imhotep the African*, we discuss the alignments of the stars Sirius and Bull's Thigh, the spring equinox risings of Sirius and Orion's Belt stars, and the tracking of the star Vega—all within a few hundred years around 6100 bce. We show how this ritual stellar science moved from the central Sahara peoples of Nabta Play to the Nile Valley circa 3300 BCE, jump-starting the pyramid-building Egyptian civilization, especially informing the great vizier Imhotep's design of the first Great Pyramid, the Step Pyramid of Saqqara for king Djoser.

At Nabta Playa a circle of knee-high stones called the "Calendar Circle" indicates the motions of Orion's Belt from 4800 BCE back to about 6300 BCE—and the device teaches about the entire precession cycle of the sky, speaking to its ancient users about two time periods—5000 BCE and half a precession cycle before then, circa 16,500 BCE, bracketing the time the ancient Egyptians as Zep Tepi, the "first time"—the origin point of civilization itself. The great pyramids at Giza, reflections of heaven on earth, also refer back to that time via their reflection of the stars of Orion's Belt, and the possible association of the Great Sphinx with the Leo constellation.

Back to the First Time: Vega and the Subterranean Passage

The stars that were tracked ceremonially at Nabta and in the early Nile Valley civilization temples were Sirius, Orion's Belt, and the circumpolar stars. Vega (Alpha Lyrae in Greek), at the very bright visual magnitude 0.0, has occupied the top of the stellar brightness scale since Hellenistic times. Vega and Arcturus are the brightest stars in the Northern Hemisphere, and Vega is by far the brightest star ever observed near the path of the celestial pole. For several centuries around 12,000 BCE, Vega was the brightest polestar—North Star— *ever*.

Consider now the Great Pyramid at Giza. From its two internal chambers, the King's Chamber and the Queen's Chamber, there originate shafts that run straight out of the pyramid right along the meridian, the north-south line in the sky. Early modern explorers called them air shafts. Today it is generally accepted that the shafts were in fact associated with stars—specifically, the southern shaft originating in the King's Chamber was oriented to Orion's Belt and the southern shaft originating in the Queen's Chamber was oriented to Sirius.

The Great Pyramid complex contains another major shaft that is oriented along the meridian line in the sky. The mysterious Subterranean Passage cuts in a straight line from the entrance of the Great Pyramid down through several layers of masonry then deep into the bedrock to a chamber right beneath the center of the massive pyramid. Despite many attempts of scholars, this major meridianal shaft has never been successfully associated with any star. There just did not seem to be an important star at the right place at the right time.

The shaft itself is truly extraordinary. The passage is 1.2 meters (about 4 feet) high and 1.04 meters (3.4 feet) wide, and runs 105 meters (344 feet) into the bedrock. It is surprisingly uniform and straight, descending at an angle of 26.52°. The passage points to a declination of 86.54° in the sky, 3.46° directly south of the celestial north pole. It is precisely aligned over its entire length, "without deviating more than a centimeter in angle or orientation," as Egyptologist Mark Lehner puts it (*The Complete Pyramids*, London: Thames and Hudson, 1997). In his *Pyramids and Temples of Gizeh*, meticulous pyramid surveyor Sir Flinders Petrie notes an even greater precision for 2/5 of its length, requiring "readings to 1/100th inch or to one arc second on the longer distances." It is one of the most astonishingly precise features of the whole Great Pyramid complex. It points to the sky. To what else could it be oriented other than something in the heavens? The passage is cut so consistently straight and so precisely, that surely the 3.46° deviation from the pole is intentional.

To what could this passage have been oriented? Because in my book *The Origin Map* I discussed megalithic constructions at Nabta oriented to Vega, I tested Vega against the Giza passage. Employing current measures for Vega's proper motion (SIMBAD at the Strasbourg Astronomical Data Center) and calculating Earth's pole movement, we see that Vega achieved its highest declination of 86.54° around 12,070 BCE—exactly aligned with the Giza passage! And not at some random date, but exactly at northern culmination, the closest Vega ever comes to the celestial pole in its 26,000-year precession cycle. Given the height and length of the shaft, its viewing angle ranges from declinations of 86.22° to 86.87°, centered on 86.54°. Vega would have begun shining down to the bottom of the passage about 12,320 BCE, hitting the center of the shaft 12,070 BCE, until 11,820 BCE, when it disappeared from the shaft. This Vega-shaft "coincidence" is also in the general Zep Tepi time frame as referred to by the ancient Egyptians.

Importantly Sirius also culminated at about the same time. Robert Bauvals in *The Egypt Code*, notes that at Zep Tepi, Sirius was just visible on the horizon as seen from the Giza plateau. Let us consider this Sirius connection in more detail. Employing the latest measures and calculations, we see that Sirius reached its southern culmination around 12,280 BCE at a declination of −60.43°, which is the horizon at Giza looking south. The geometric horizon is −60.02°, and the visual horizon corrected for atmospheric refraction is about −60.5°. Thus, the Giza plateau is the sole place on Earth (the only latitude) where Sirius at its southernmost culmination just barely eclipses the horizon.

At that time Sirius was only glimpsed at the horizon at midnight around the summer solstice. The Giza plateau was a perfect viewing location for that epochal event—marking the Zep Tepi, or first time, perhaps precisely when Giza originally became a sacred site. At locations north Sirius disappears completely for centuries, whereas at locations south Sirius never vanishes. At the same time brilliant Vega was the north polestar shining down the center of the Subterranean Passage. (A note on the visual versus the geometric horizon: The visual horizon is about 0.5 degrees lower than the geometric horizon because starlight is bent as it passes through Earth's atmosphere, so one can see starlight from slightly below the geometric horizon. The precise amount depends on temperature and humidity, but generally it is about 0.5°.)

A PREHISTORIC JOURNEY TO THE FIRST TIME

Sirius is so bright it is the only star that can be seen during the daytime. At night it is sighted as soon as it breaks the horizon. Imagine you are living in Egypt circa 12,250 BCE. You are highly attuned to the night sky, especially the brightest star of all, Sirius. It is near the summer solstice, and it is millennia before the monsoons will move north to bring life again to the desert, so you choose to stay near the life-sustaining waters of the Nile.

A well-conditioned wanderer, you travel north for several days one hot summer, about 55 kilometers (34 miles) per day. This distance is half of one degree latitude on Earth's surface. You are five days' walk south of the place that is now called Giza. The always-easy-to-spot asterism of Orion's Belt rises early in the evening in the far southeast, and culminates in the south, hanging at a low altitude of 15° two hours before midnight. Exactly 110 minutes before midnight, Orion's trailing companion, the starry ruler of the night sky, Sirius, cracks the horizon 12° east of due south and skims the southern horizon very low, reaching altitude of just 2° before falling below the horizon. But if you climb a low hill or dune in the desert you can view your old friend Sirius for a couple of hours around midnight. To the north the brilliant Vega is always visible at night, restlessly traveling a tight circle about 3.5° from the celestial pole.

As you trek north each day the starry show in the night repeats, but Sirius skims the horizon lower and for a shorter amount of time each night. By the time you arrive at Giza Sirius makes such a low, brief arc on the horizon that viewing it requires perfectly clear conditions, and you must stand on a platform to catch even a glimpse. A few more days' walk farther north it will be impossible to glimpse Sirius at all. Such star tracking is deeply ingrained in your ancestral lore and your marking of time. Daytime's angle of the sun in the sky informs you the time of year, and at night the appearance of Sirius tells you the same. What's more, you know that farther north, earlier generations were able to glimpse Sirius before it disappeared entirely from their sky. Your ancestors have been studying the sky for so long, they can teach you how the sky changes over a very long time. Thus you know Sirius will once again return to the northern regions, that the brilliant Vega will move down away from the celestial pole, and that Sirius will climb higher in the sky once again. That is why the place in which you are standing now is the place of the first time, Zep Tepi: Giza.

DUAL DATING AND THE REVIVAL OF EXTREME ANTIQUITY

The ancient name of the Great Pyramid at Giza, the Egyptian name, was Akhet Khufu, meaning the "horizon of Khufu" (Lehner,

The Complete Pyramids). Is it possible that the sacred place where Khufu marshaled his kingdom to build the Great Pyramid was already known simply as Akhet, the "horizon," the place on Earth where the ruler of heaven, Sirius, briefly comes down exactly to rest on the horizon every 26,000 years? Obviously it was already a very ancient sacred site.

The layout of the Giza pyramids reflect the stars of Orion's Belt alluding to a distant past and symbolically referencing the Zep Tepi origin time described in inscriptions, as well as the southern culmination of Sirius and the northern culmination of Vega. Similarly, the Calendar Circle at Nabta Playa, constructed and used circa 5000 BCE, teaches about even earlier times—about the entire precession cycle, in fact. And there is evidence that megaliths and bedrock sculptures at Nabta were maintained over several thousand years (see *Black Genesis*).

Sacred sites around the world are built and rebuilt on earlier constructions, often spanning millennia. Many scholars have suggested the Giza plateau is one such site. Probably the most stunning evidence for this came from Boston University geologist Robert Schoch, who, together with independent Egyptologist John Anthony West, measured the weathering of the Great Sphinx and its enclosure. Schoch essentially proved from a geophysical standpoint the Sphinx was weathered by long-term heavy rainfall and thus pre-dates 5000 BCE. Although we cannot measure precisely when the Sphinx was carved into the living bedrock, his analysis yields 5000 BCE as a *minimum* age.

Like all discoveries that challenge a reigning dogma, Schoch's dating of the Sphinx continues to generate voluminous polemical argumentation, but he is well-supported by the geophysical evidence. A common complaint against Schoch's dating of the Sphinx was stated by Zahi Hawass, director of the Supreme Council of Antiquities in Egypt: "But no single piece of material culture, not a single object nor piece of an object, has been found at Giza that can be interpreted as coming from a lost civilization [before the Egyptian Dynasties]" (from the preface to Siliotti). But during the past 15 years astonishing revelations from an archaeological site in Anatolia Turkey called Gobekli Tepe confound the claimants that there could not have been earlier monument building cultures. Dating to at least the tenth millennium BCE, and probably earlier, the people of Gobekli Tepe were building exquisitely carved massive stone pillars arranged in rings, featuring animal motifs probably with astrological meaning and with astronomical orientation. There exists exquisite ancient rock art, such as that of the Lascaux caves in France, dating to 15,000 BCE, which, although not monumental architecture, contains probable astroceremonial motifs. Thus Egyptologists Lehner and Hawass's claims that older symbolic architecture at Giza is impossible because there was none in the world, are now essentially moot.

I suggest there may have been symbolic architecture on the Giza plateau as far back as the *actual* Zep Tepi, including the Subterranean Passage and Chamber, beneath a mound topped by a flat platform at the level where the Queen's Chamber exists today. Indeed it is well known that the Great Pyramid was built over a bedrock mound platform 8 meters (26 feet) high that extends to where the Subterranean Passage emerges from the bedrock (Siliotti). Given this, the Great Pyramid was built in the Fourth Dynasty on top of the then-ancient Subterranean Passage and platform. The Zep Tepi platform is symbolically present in the horizontal passage that leads to the Queen's Chamber. It has the same dimensions (1.2 meters [3.9 feet] in height) as the Subterranean Passage, and serves as another meridianal star shaft directed exactly along the horizon—symbolically preserving the much more ancient platform used at Zep Tepi, the first time, and preserving the place on Earth that demarcates the parts of Earth where Sirius always lives and the parts of Earth where Sirius disappears.

Further symbolic unity with deep antiquity is the *ascending* passage that connects the Subterranean Passage and the horizontal passage of the Queen's Chamber. It is of the same dimensions (1.2 meters [3.9 feet] in height), and is sloped upward at an identical angle to the downward slope of the Subterranean Passage—much like a reflection off the horizon. On the Sirius platform at Zep Tepi, it was possible for a single priest or priestess using a simple flat reflector or still pool of water to connect the light of Vega of the north shining down the passage to the light of Sirius of the south as it just skimmed the horizon. Thus two great rulers of the starry sky—Sirius, the crown jewel of the night, and Vega, the ruler of all polestars—were united simultaneously. Their precise culminations were 180 years apart, but for centuries, about 12,020 BCE, they simultaneously shone along the horizon platform and into the Subterranean Passage. Significantly this starry drama occurred at midnight when the sky was darkest, only for a few days around summer solstice—a festival perennially important to cultures throughout time. And the Giza plateau slopes down and away to the southeast for a perfect view of the starry show.

In ancient Egypt the heliacal reappearance of Sirius marked the new year and the imminent arrival of the Nile floods, much as it marked the playa-filling monsoons at Nabta. Monuments simultaneously marking the rising Sirius and the circumpolar stars celebrate the bounteous measure of the new-year cycle. At the place of the first time, Zep Tepi, the start of the new Great Year of precessional motion of Sirius is monumentally indicated, as is the cycle of the celestial pole by the greatest polestar of all, Vega. There is an elegant similarity/complimentarity in this symbolic stellar equation of the annual cycle and the Great Year cycle of the ages.

ANOTHER SHAFT TO THE SKY

Scientifically speaking, the Vega alignment is only one star on one line and therefore not statistically significant. But it represents a symbolism repeated again and again, and occurs at the special time of culmination. Still, objectors would say other examples of the same alignment are needed for verification. So let us examine other such subterranean passages.

In fact, there is one at another of the six giant pyramids of Egypt. The six, according to Lehner, are: Third Dynasty king Djoser's Step Pyramid at Saqqara, Fourth Dynastry founder Sneferu's Bent Pyramid and Red Pyramid at Dashur, the great pyramids of Khufu and Khafre at Giza, and the Fourth Dynasty Unfinished Pyramid at Za-wiyet el-Aryan. Sneferu's Bent Pyramid at Dashur has a long, precise subterranean passage shaft. Located 21 kilometers (13 miles) south of Giza, the giant Bent Pyramid is at latitude 29.79°. We learn from Egyptologist I.E.S. Edwards that the passage starts at the north en-trance to the pyramid, 12 meters (39 feet) above ground. It continues down through the masonry for 25 meters (82 feet), first at an angle of 28.36°, then shifting to an angle of 26.33° before moving into the bedrock for another 48 meters (157 feet). The passage continues straight to a chamber under the center of the pyramid, and the en-tire length of the passage into the bedrock is at a constant angle of 26.33°. This angle, combined with its latitude, points to a location in the sky with a precise declination of 86.54° —identical to the Subter-ranean Passage of the Great Pyramid of Khufu at Giza. So if this shaft existed at Zep Tepi, plunging into the bedrock beneath a ho-rizon-viewing platform on the surface, a similar starry drama could have been observed at Dashur—the only difference being at Dashur, Sirius would rise to a slightly higher altitude by about 20 arc minutes.

The ancient name of the Bent Pyramid meant the "southern shin-ing pyramid" (Lehner). Perhaps, when Sneferu marshaled his king-dom to build the Bent Pyramid, the location was already known and revered as the southern shining—the place on Earth where the ruler of the heavens, Sirius, shines eternally and never disappears beneath the horizon. Sneferu's names for his three large pyramids further enhance the story. The first, at Meidum, bears an exalted personal name: "Sneferu endures." The last, north of the southern pyramid, had the ancient name "Shining pyramid." The Bent Pyramid and its subterranean passage are also located such that the southern horizon is flat, thus affording excellent viewing of the starry drama. So the only two long, precise subterranean passages under the true giant pyramids were oriented to the same location in the sky, evidence that the builders indeed had astronomical intent.

The two other great pyramids on the Giza plateau, of Menkaure and Khafre, have shorter, less surgically precise subterranean passages, but they are still consistent with the same basic location in the sky. Menkaure's descends 31 meters (102 feet), half through courses of masonry and then into the bedrock at an angle of 26.03°, and Khafre's passage descends a much shorter distance at an angle of 25.92°. These yield declinations to the sky of about half a degree lower than that of their Great Pyramid partner, with broader angular spread of their openings, and so could have also captured the light of the culminating Vega.

Finally consider the curious dual nature of the Bent Pyramid. First there is the bend in the slope of the pyramid itself. And the northerly descending entrance passage is bent inside the masonry of the lower pyramid (which is not bent), and the west entry passage is bent from 30.15° to 24.28° inside the lower courses of masonry (Edwards, page 86). Many Egyptologists believe the Bent Pyramid was bent by accident and through poor planning, but there is ample evidence that it was planned into its structure. As Schoch puts it:

> I suspect strongly that the Bent Pyramid was meant to be bent from the beginning. Unlike any other Egyptian pyramid, it expresses duality—two angles, two geometries, two tunnel and chamber complexes. There is something ritualistic and symbolic in this shape, a meaning we now find elusive. The Egyptians clearly found this meaning to be important. The craftsmanship of the Bent Pyramid achieves a high level, and the entire structure is beautifully wrought. Clearly Sneferu and the Egyptians of his time were using architecture to express something of great importance, and they were giving this work their all (Schoch, page 27).

The Bent Pyramid is the first true giant pyramid created by the ancient Egyptians under the reign of Sneferu, founder of the Fourth Dynasty. The duality symbolism repeatedly built into the Bent Pyramid may represent the dual times—Zep Tepi (the first time) and the second time of the revival of monumental architecture in Sneferu's Fourth Dynasty. This dualistic astroceremonial architecture is also present at Giza, and it was present at Nabta Playa, representing the Great Year cycle of the ages and the annual cycle of seasons—the southern culmination of Sirius at midnight during the summer solstice and the star's heliacal reappearance at dawn.

Any new interpretation, such as the one I proffer here, if it will endure the test of time, usually has some folklore, mythology, or story from the past associated with it, ignored by moderns. In this case a literature search found the work of Manly P. Hall, who wrote in 1928: "In the light of the secret philosophy of the Egyptian initiates, W.W. Harmon...determines that the first ceremonial of the Pyramid was performed 68,890 years ago on the occasion when the star Vega for the first time sent its ray down the descending passage into the pit." W.W. Harmon was an esoteric Theosophist who claimed to have received telepathically from an ancient initiatory tradition, the basic idea of Vega shining down the passage as the first use of the Giza complex. Interestingly Harmon was correct about Vega, but he was completely wrong in his date calculations.

THE SEQUENCE OF EVENTS

Circa 12,000 BCE, a largely unknown culture of people in the region of north Africa carefully followed the sky, especially Sirius and north polestars, as part of their religion, culture, and science. They employed tremendous effort to dig and sculpt subterranean passages in the bedrock and surface viewing/ceremonial platforms at Giza and Dashur. Possibly the Great Sphinx was also constructed for this purpose. Then, with the end of the Ice Age, climate change caused the Sahara desert to bloom, as rains returned to the region and the peoples migrated there from the Nile. Gradually over the next several thousand years, these African star people of the Sahara became the forerunner of the Egyptian civilization, building the astroceremonial complex at Nabta Playa. When the monsoon pattern again drifted south and extreme dryness returned to the Sahara, they moved to the Nile Valley and developed the archaic temple of Satis at Elephantine Island and spread throughout the Nile Valley, assimilating the local populations into dynastic Egypt and increasing their megalithic building activities. By the Third Dynasty, King Djoser, with his astronomer-priest and great vizier, Imhotep, built at Saqqara the first major monumental complex of dynastic Egypt featuring the same stars (Sirius and the polestars). Then Fourth Dynasty founder King Sneferu and his son, King Khufu, built the Bent Pyramid at Dashur, followed by the Great Pyramid at Giza. These were purposefully constructed on top of much more ancient sacred subterranean passages and platforms from Zep Tepi. Thus all the truly monumental pyramid architecture of the dynastic period is associated symbolically with Zep Tepi. Whether the Dynastic kings rediscovered the sacred site at Giza or whether knowledge of it was maintained throughout the ages, we can't know for sure. But one thing is certain: They wrote about the Shemsu Hor, the Followers of Horus, the ancestors and great kings of the mythical time of Zep Tepi.

Sothic Cycles and Zep Tepi

The ancient Egyptians used an annual civil calendar of 365 days, but the astronomical year is about 365 and 1/4 days. For whatever reason, they did not correct for the missing 1/4 day with leap-year calendars, as we do. So their civil calendar drifted steadily against the backdrop of the astronomical cycles. Important astronomical festival dates, especially the annual reappearance of Sirius to herald the life-sustaining floods of the Nile, drifted against the civil calendar, resynchronizing every 1,460 years in what is called a Sothic cycle. The only existing documented synchronized date of the reappearance of

Sirius with the first day of Thoth New Year's festival occurred in 139 CE. Because the precession motion of stars causes the precise duration of a Sothic cycle to deviate some number of years from the simplified 1,460, there has always been some dispute among scholars as to the Sothic calendar re-synchronization dates in ancient times. Consider all the way back to circa 12,000 BCE, when Sirius was very low on the southern horizon and didn't even reach to 1° altitude. Simple geometry shows us a very interesting fact: When Sirius was at its southern culmination it was highest in the sky at midnight on the summer solstice. At Giza, the place of Zep Tepi, the precise year about 12,000 BCE marking the southern culmination of Sirius was by definition the heliacal rise of the entire Sirius precession cycle—the origin of the supercycle of all the cycles. Further, at essentially the same time the queen of all polestars, Vega, culminated, shining down into the Subterranean Passage, and the pattern of the three stars of Orion's belt matched the pattern of the three pyramids of Giza, and perhaps the Sphinx gazed at the rising of Leo due east.

ANCIENT EVIDENCE MEETS A MODERN SOFTWARE GLITCH

These ancient calculations encounter current professional astronomy as follows: I calculated the Vega-Shaft alignment using the published astrophysical literature, and we first published it in our book *Black Genesis*. Then, in April 2013, while hosting an "author of the month" forum at GrahamHancock.com, I learned that the popular astronomical calculation program StarryNight Pro gave a slightly different location for Vega at that ancient date. StarryNight showed Vega culminating north at declination 86.24° in 12,008 BCE, which is 0.299° less than my value. I calculated Vega's ancient motion using the Earth's pole movement equations published in astrophysical journals. I calculated the values myself instead of using a canned program such as StarryNight, because when I began extreme antiquity calculations circa 1999, the available software used a poor

approximation for such extreme ancient stellar dating. Today StarryNight's values are much improved. I contacted StarryNight about
this and they responded that I had "found an error" in their ancient
precession calculations, and they kindly offered to send me a beta
version of the fix that they were working on. As of this writing they
have not yet released their correction. If it turns out that the current StarryNight value for ancient Vega is more accurate than my
value, the situation is only slightly altered. The center of the Subterranean Passage is declination 86.544°; the edges of the shaft to the
outside of today's Pyramid are 86.2825° and 86.8052°. So if Vega
culminated at 86.24007°, the StarryNight value, it just missed shining down by 0.04° if the shaft angle did not shift geophysically over
the past 14,000 years (and that is a separate issue). But the whole
pyramid was not there around 12,000 BCE; only the underground part
of the shaft was. Its edges are at declinations 86.187° and 86.900°.
So if StarryNight's current value turns out to be correct, then Vega
started shining to the bottom of the bedrock shaft circa 12,120 BCE,

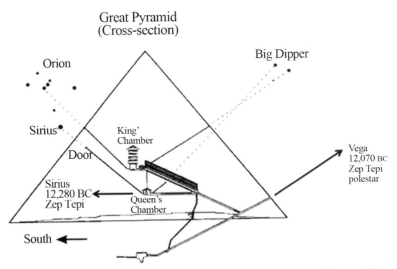

Subterranean passage and internal platform indicate Zep Tepi. Above-ground
shafts indicate the Old Kingdom. Diagram adapted from Black Genesis.

and continued shining down the shaft through its culmination 12,008 until 11,896 BCE, when Vega's declination descended too low to shine down for another 26,000 years.

THE BIG QUESTION: WHY?

Why would such early structures emphasize the stars? Clearly the actual and practical significance of the annual reappearance of Sirius heralding the annual rains extended back in time before dynastic Egypt to the Nabta Playa culture and possibly earlier. Generally, the earliest religious and ceremonial practices around the world incorporated star lore into their central beliefs. The religious principle "as above, so below" came from ancient Egypt, and Egypt was considered to be a model of heaven on Earth. And perhaps there are deeper reasons, more difficult for us to understand. Ancient Eastern religions believed in long-term *yuga cycles* for the development of human consciousness; these cycles were possibly associated with the astronomical precession cycle, similar to the Western concept of Zodiac ages. Could these ancient structures be telling us something about an actual connection of humanity to the cosmos, in ways that our currently dominant material worldview cannot comprehend? For now that will have to remain a mystery.

REFERENCES

Bauval, Robert, and Thomas Brophy. *Black Genesis: The Prehistoric Origins of Ancient Egypt.* Vermont: Bear & Co. 2011.

———. *Imhotep the African: Architect of the Cosmos.* Newburyport, Mass.: RedWheel/Weiser, 2013.

Brophy, Thomas. *The Origin Map: Discovery of a Prehistoric Megalithic Astrophysical Map and Sculpture of the Universe.* Bloomington, Ind.: iUniverse, 2002.

Edwards, I.E.S. *The Pyramids of Egypt.* Middlesex: Penguin. 1955.

Hall, Manly P. *The Secret Teachings of All Ages*. Radford, Va.: Wilder, 2007.

Lehner, Mark. *The Complete Pyramids*. London: Thames and Hudson, 1997.

Petrie, W.M.F. *The Pyramids and Temples of Gizeh*. London: n.p., 1883.

Schoch, R.M., and R.A. McNally. *Pyramid Quest*. New York: Penguin, 2005.

Siliotti, Alberto. *Guide to the Pyramids of Egypt*. New York: Barnes and Noble Books, 1997.

SIMBAD Astronomical Database: *http://simbad.u-strasbg.fr/simbad/simid?*

The Ancient Astronaut Theory: An Indigenous Perspective

By Ardy Sixkiller Clarke

Ever since Roswell, stories of UFOs and alien beings have become almost commonplace. But are these stories really new, or have they been common throughout history? Are there extant ancient records of aliens—Star People—that visited Earth in the distant past? According to the oral traditions of many indigenous people from the Americas, Australia, New Zealand, the South Pacific, Africa, Scandinavia, and Polynesia, there are. Indigenous people around the world have safeguarded stories, customs, and ceremonies that allude to or incorporate references to such Star People. Most hold those traditions as part of their religion or at least as a part of their ancient history. Some even believe their creation is tied to ancestors from the stars and report regular communication and collaboration with the Star People. While most scientists have discarded such ideas as the made-up stories of superstitious peoples, I now believe, after my extensive travels among and interactions with various indigenous and native tribes, that there must be something more to their legends and traditions than that. The fact is that many indigenous peoples acknowledge UFO encounters as part of their reality and speak, in their myths and legends, of beings that came from the sky or the stars.

OVERVIEW OF THE THEORY

Indigenous stories differ somewhat from the ancient astronaut theories of contemporary writers, and I will examine those contemporary theories in the context of indigenous oral literature and history. Ancient astronaut theorists contend that highly advanced extraterrestrials landed on earth thousands of years ago and were mistaken as gods by the primitive ancient cultures they encountered. These theorists advance the idea that the human race is actually the creation of these extraterrestrial beings, and that they built, or at least assisted in the construction of, the Egyptian and Maya pyramids, the Moai stones on Rapa Nui (Easter Island), and the Nazca Lines of Peru, among many other ancient structures and sites. Another aspect of this theory is that much of human culture, religion, and knowledge comes from these extraterrestrial travelers.

Proponents base their hypothesis on two types of evidence: (1) petroglyphs depicting alien-like figures on ancient architectural structures and other ancient wonders; and (2) religious texts that describe interactions with gods and other heavenly beings with amazing, superhuman powers who descended from the sky in vehicles of fire. Embedded within the theory is the idea that these extraterrestrial visitor-scientists manipulated the DNA of primates for the purpose of improving the human species and accelerating the process of civilization here on earth. Once they were able to isolate the DNA elements, they cloned the forerunners of the human species. A more moderate hypothesis maintains that the extraterrestrial Sky Gods arrived on earth and taught indigenous peoples how to build pyramids, cities, and other marvelous structures. Other supposed evidence of the existence of these extraterrestrials includes anachronistic archaeological artifacts that were presumed superior to the technical capabilities of the ancient cultures that produced them, as well as traditional legends that account for or obliquely describe extraterrestrial contact. Despite the popularity of these ideas, most scientists and academics regard them as pseudo-archaeology.

EARLY PROPONENTS

Erich von Däniken, who published the best-selling *Chariots of the Gods?* in 1968, is most often considered the father of the ancient astronaut theory (AAT), though earlier writers proposed similar theories long before von Däniken came on the scene. However, von Däniken gave little or no credit to these authors, authors that included Charles Fort (1919); Harold Wilkins (1954); Morris K. Jessup (1955); George Hunt Williamson (1957); Peter Kolosimo (1957); Henri Lhote (1958), Matest M. Agrest (1959); Jacques Bergier and Louis Pauwels (1960); Brinsley Le Poer Trench (1960); Paul Misraki (1962); W. Raymond Drake (1964); and I.S. Shklovskii and Carl Sagan (1966). The general consensus, however, is that the theory originated with von Däniken.

Charles Fort, who wrote *Book of the Damned* (1919), is actually regarded as the first ufologist. The title of his book refers to what Holt called the "damned" data, which had been damned, or excluded, by close-minded scientists because said data did not conform to accepted guidelines. Fort believed that academics did not search for the truth if it was contrary to what they believed. Rejecting mainstream thought, Holt wrote about such events as teleportation (a term he is credited with coining), anachronistic artifacts (out-of-place artifacts), unidentified flying objects, and extraterrestrial visitors to earth (ancient astronauts). In his 1923 book, *New Lands*, Fort speculated that these extraterrestrial beings might have even kidnapped humans (alien abduction). Fort's theories are thought to be responsible for the incessant controversy over, awe and mystification regarding, fabrications regarding, mockery of, and, occasionally, serious investigation of UFOs during the 45 years following the publication of his book.

CONTEMPORARY ADVOCATES

The power of the media, the motion picture industry, television, and eventually the Internet accorded the UFO phenomenon unprecedented public visibility in the latter half of the 20th century. While it is not clear what percentage of the public believe in the AAT, the History Channel has contributed immensely to prevailing attitudes toward the theory with its TV series *Ancient Aliens*. In fact, critics of the series have noted that because the majority of Americans obtain information from television, and because the very word *history* implies truth, the series has contributed substantially to the acceptance of the AAT. In fact, a recent National Geographic study reported that 78 per cent of the public believes that aliens exist and visit planet earth.

The AAT also gained momentum during the last half of the 20th century through the works of contemporary writers such as Erich von Däniken, Zecharia Sitchin, and Robert K.G. Temple, all of whom have appeared on the History Channel's *Ancient Alien* series. As previously noted, Swiss author Erich von Däniken wrote *Chariots of the Gods?* which became an immediate bestseller. In it, he puts forth the hypothesis that thousands of years ago, extraterrestrials visited earth and taught humans about technology and influenced ancient religions. He argues that the great cities of the Maya and the stone relics of the Incas were constructed under the influence of these space visitors. He also maintains that both ancient writings of biblical prophets and cave drawings provide evidence of encounters with extraterrestrials in that their creation required a more sophisticated technological ability than was available to the ancient cultures that created them. Von Däniken maintains that these artifacts were constructed either directly by extraterrestrial visitors or by humans who were assisted by the space travelers. He further claims that geographically separated ancient cultures shared artistic themes, which, he argues, implies a common origin. Since the appearance of von Däniken's *Chariots*, more than 300 books advancing the AAT have been written; von Däniken himself has defended his theories with a series of books, despite the fact that scientists, theologians, and archaeologists have rallied to demonstrate the fallacy of his claims.

One of the more influential theorists of alien visitation is Zechariah Sitchin, who bases his ideas on texts such as the Sumerian *Epic of Gilgamesh,* the *Enuma Elish,* Homer's *Odyssey,* and the Hebrew Bible. Sitchin's series, *The Earth Chronicles,* beginning with *The 12th Planet,* revolves around Sitchin's unique interpretation of ancient Sumerian and Middle Eastern texts, and artifacts from around the world. He believes that the gods of Mesopotamia were astronauts from the planet Nibiru, the 12th planet. According to Sitchin, Nibiru continues to orbit our sun on a 3,600-year elongated orbit. Even though there is no scientific evidence to support this idea, Sitchin's Nibiru has a tremendous following as evidenced by the number of Websites, authors, and bloggers discussing the "ghost planet" online. Sitchin also claims that some Sumerian texts tell the story of 50 *Anunnaki,* inhabitants of Nibiru who came to Earth approximately 400,000 years ago with the intent of mining gold for transport back to their home planet. While on Earth they genetically engineered laborers to work the mines, thereby creating *Homo sapiens,* which he calls *Adapa,* the Adam of the biblical texts. Sitchin asserts that the Anunnaki were active in human affairs until their culture was destroyed by global catastrophe, leaving Earth only after giving humans the opportunity and means to govern themselves.

NATIVE AMERICAN PERSPECTIVES

In the 2003 anniversary edition of *God Is Red,* noted Ogallala Sioux scholar Vine Deloria, Jr. addresses the humanity of Native people in an added chapter to the original edition, titled "Natural and Hybrid Peoples." In this chapter, he examines the AAT popularized by Erich von Däniken. While he rejects von Däniken's hypothesis, he suggests that Zecharia Sitchin, in his *Earth Chronicles* quartet, advances this idea of ancient visitations in a responsible and comprehensive way. He acknowledges that some of Sitchin's ideas are questionable, though Deloria suggests that there appears to be some truth in his theories. At this point, however, in a tongue-in-cheek manner,

Deloria turns the AAT upside down by declaring that the proponents of ancient astronaut visitation have one crucial fact wrong: It was not the Indians of the Americas that these extraterrestrials visited and intermarried with, but the Europeans. Believing that the AAT is an insult on America's Native population, Deloria asserts that it was not indigenous people, but Westerners who were influenced by the aliens. Deloria explains that an extraterrestrial influence can explain important and unique aspects of Western thought and culture. For example, only Westerners embraced inflexible, hierarchical constructs of society, and orderly and linear concepts of time, both of which were common in technologically advanced societies. Thus, these differences must be the result of alien influences and cultures.

Historically, the link between Native Americans and extraterrestrials went unnoticed until the 1970s. Scholars have traced that interest to altered attitudes about sacred sites, attitudes that gained popularity through various disciplines, including archaeology, astronomy, and anthropology. Almost overnight, indigenous holy places became centers of mysterious spiritual forces connected to alien ancestors. Suddenly, American Indian spirituality was rooted in the science of superior ancient civilizations founded by star travelers. Interest in ancient knowledge originated with the study of European sites such as Stonehenge, where scholars noted that the arrangements of the stones were aligned to astronomical events such as the rising and setting of the sun and the solstices. American archaeologists reported similar alignments in the Americas. Sites such as the Big Horn Medicine Wheel in Wyoming, Chichén Itza in Mexico, the Nazca lines in Peru, Cahokia in Illinois, and Chaco Canyon in New Mexico seemed to indicate sophisticated astronomical knowledge on the part of their creators. This emerging field of *archeoastronomy* coincided with the popularization of UFO research in the 1960s and 1970s. As well, through the work of such authors as Erich Von Däniken, who proposed that there was ample evidence of UFOs in the cultures of the Mayas and Incas, interest in ancient aliens and Star People grew.

Virtually all indigenous cultures transmit stories of encounters with Star People or Sky Gods. There is a prevailing assumption that indigenous peoples have had ongoing relationships with Star People and have been receiving regular messages and visits from them. The origin of this assumption is often based upon a modern form of mysticism that blends reality with the magical and the spiritual. While Native nations as a rule have not been forthcoming about their connections to UFOs, Star People, or Sky Gods, or about their knowledge of aliens, there has been some movement in that direction.

In 1996 a small group of Sioux (Lakota, Dakota, and Nakota) Indians and some non-Native promoters sponsored the first Star Knowledge Conference on the Yankton Sioux Indian Reservation, the homeland of a subgroup of the Dakota Sioux tribe in South Dakota. The purpose of the conference was to share with Western society the knowledge of the Star People that these indigenous people had, up until that time, kept secret. The conference was not totally welcomed within the Indian community. There were protests by dissenting groups during each day of the conference. The resistance to sharing traditions outside their own culture is not new, but Standing Elk, a Lakota Sioux, ignored the protests and maintained that he had been commanded in a vision to share his knowledge of the Star People with the people of the world. He also related being visited by "gray beings" and Star Visitors in a sweat lodge. Several other indigenous leaders in attendance suggested that the conference itself was a fulfillment of ancient tribal prophecies. Many participants claimed they participated in response to signs they had received. These signs reportedly informed them that the time had come to share their oral traditions, including the origin of their people in the stars and the influence of Star People on the formation of their respective cultures. Rod Shenandoah, a Blackfeet-Oneida elder, said that his people considered themselves privileged to be visited privately by the Star People during the present day. Holy men and elders from Maya, Choctaw, Hopi, Iroquois, Oneida, Seneca, Yaqui, Maori, and Sami nations participated alongside such featured speakers as Steven Greer, Whitley Strieber, Leo Sprinkle, Richard Boylan, John Mack, and other non-Natives who are well-known researchers in the field of ufology. Despite the initial pushback, the conference is now held annually at different locations around the country.

Throughout the conference, all of the speakers, regardless of tribal affiliation, spoke of warnings from the Star People regarding the condition of the Earth. Oglala spiritual advisor Floyd Hand spoke of *avatars* (world religious teachers) such as Jesus, Buddha, Muhammad, and White Buffalo Calf Woman, the woman who brought the Lakota their spiritual knowledge and ceremonial practices. He said that seven different galaxies were represented on Earth and that each American Indian tribe had its own extraterrestrial race of origin. He predicted major changes for the Earth and spoke of four omens. Hand said that the first of these omens would involve the birth of a white buffalo calf on a white man's ranch whose hide would eventually turn the other colors of the Four Nations (yellow, red, and black). The second omen would be heralded by the birth of another white buffalo calf, this time to a Lakota rancher. The third omen would be the birth of a third white buffalo that would attract little attention. And, finally, the fourth omen would be the actual return of the Star People. In response to these omens, he urged people to plant gardens and store food, predicting that a new government would come to power and that the fourth world would end on January 21, 2021.

Origin Legends

At the fist Star Knowledge Conference, Standing Elk discussed Lakota origin legends that pinpointed the Pleiades, Sirius, and Orion as the cosmological locations of the tribe's origins. At a subsequent conference in Las Cruces, New Mexico, Rod Skenedore, a native elder and Indian rights activist, maintained that humanity was "seeded" on Earth by the Star People. Kenneth Meadows, a best-selling author on shamanic wisdom, noted how various tribes talk about having come to their historical homeland from some other place, perhaps another world entirely. He further stated that the ancient teachings of the Cherokee maintain that they came to Earth 250,000 years ago from a planet near the star Sirius, and that the tribe retained the language of their home planet.

Harley Swiftdeer Reagan, the founder of the Deer Tribe Metis Medicine Society, claimed that the Cherokee descended from Star People who arrived from another planetary system almost a million years ago. Other Cherokee stories describe how the Star People created *Elohi* (Earth) for the Cherokee people. The Skidi band of Pawnee still design their lodges and villages so that they are in alignment with the stars and planets. They do this because in their creation narrative, Mars, the red morning star warrior, marries Venus, the female evening star, to produce the first humans. The Cree claim they came from the stars in spirit form and became flesh and blood. And finally, Osage legends maintain that some Osage lived in the sky in a place far from Earth, before they moved to Earth and made it their home.

South American Narratives

The Shipibo Indians, who live in the Ucayali River basin of east-central Peru, believe that seven Star Children were the ancestors of all the Amazon's indigenous people. At the end of their lives, the children returned to the stars and became *Huishmabu*, a constellation that helps the Shipibo chart the course of the year and is the inspiration for and source of the geometric designs found in their artwork. The Yagua Indians of the Peruvian Amazon, known for their skill with the blowgun, still practice their ancient ceremonies, the central god or spiritual being of which is Mayantu, who is said to descend from the sky during celebrations held in his honor.

In Brazil, indigenous tribal people speak of travelers from the sky who descended to earth when humans were little more than animals, to instruct them in agriculture, astronomy, and medicine. One being in particular, Bep-Kororoti, a space warrior worshipped as a god, possessed a flying vehicle capable of destroying anything in its path. Bep-Kororoti is said to have terrified the natives until he revealed himself to be a fair-skinned man. He supposedly amused the natives with his magic until he grew restless for his home in the sky, at which point he left, never to return. Anthropologist Bernardo Ipupiara, who works at the Smithsonian Institute, is a member of the *Uru-e Wau-Wau* tribe in the state of Para in northern Brazil. Llyn Roberts, in his book *Shaman From the Stars*, describes *huskerahs* (a *huskerah* is a soundless device from the sky that is not a bird) that landed in the Amazon Basin. *Makuras*, small glowing beings with large eyes who came in the *huskerahs*, taught the *Uru-e Wau-Wau* how to plant seeds and grow corn. According to Ipupiara, engravings of *atojars* ("entities that come from the sky") can be found on cave walls. He said the beings left when the Great Spirit told them they were needed elsewhere, but the people are still waiting for the Star People to return. According to Roberts, the Uru-e Wau-Wau, which literally means "people from the stars," came from the Pleiades.

In the Columbia Amazon, the Desana, an Indian tribe of approximately 1,500 people ranging from the Rio Negro basin to Amazonas, Brazil, say that in the beginning of time, their ancestors arrived on the earth in canoes from the sky. The Desana consider themselves to have a deep-seated relationship with nature and refer to themselves as "sons of the wind." They believe that their wisdom is deeply entrenched in the astronomical traditions of their ancestors from the sky.

Likewise, the Waroa Indians, who live in the Orinoco Valley of Venezuela, believe they once lived in the sky when the earth was devoid of humans. In this sky-world they loved to hunt, but when they discovered that the earth was rich with game, they abandoned the sky and made earth their new home.

As you can see, origin narratives such as these are common among many indigenous societies.

LEGENDARY FIGURES: LITTLE PEOPLE, THUNDERERS, AND TRANSFORMERS

The otherworldly, alien-like characters that populate these legends and myths are as fascinating as the stories themselves. For example, the indigenous peoples of the Americas relate many legends of races of little people who live in the mountains or the woods, or near rock outcroppings. Among Great Lakes tribes, these little people are often depicted in petroglyphs as having horns and traveling in canoes. The Crow Indians of the northern plains consider the Pryor Mountains sacred because they are said to be the home of a race of little people who protect the tribe. Even today tribal members make offerings to the little people at Medicine Rock. In present-day Yucatan and Guatemala, Maya people speak of the *alux*, a small race of knee-high beings that appear to be dressed like the ancient Mayans. They believe that the *alux* are generally invisible but are able to assume physical form for purposes of communicating with or frightening humans.

According to Cherokee legend, when the Cherokee moved to the southeastern part of what is now Tennessee, they found many well-tended gardens upon their arrival, but no evidence of the people who created or cared for them. Eventually, they discovered a race of diminutive people who lived underground and came out only at night to tend the gardens. They harvested the food and took it underground to their cities. These people were small in stature, and had translucent, blue skin and large, black eyes. As the sun's rays were too harsh for them, they built their cities underground and only came out at night by the light of the moon. The Cherokee call them the "moon people" or "moon eye."

The small, blue-skinned people of Cherokee legend are not to be confused with their *Yunwi Tsunsdi*, a forest-dwelling race of little people who play a central role in traditional Cherokee stories. The Cherokee describe three types of these little people: the Rock People, the Laurel People, and the Dogwood People. The Rock People are vengeful and steal children; the Laurel People play tricks and are generally mischievous; and the Dogwood People are helpers and healers. Jacques Vallée discussed these legends in his book *Passport to Magnoia* and described how the little people abducted pregnant women and young mothers and even seized young children, sometimes leaving one of their own children in their place. The Cherokee called such children *changelings* or *transformers*, as they had the ability to transform the land and create arable farmland out of moving mountains and rivers in these tales.

Both the Iroquois and the Cherokee tell of the supernatural powers of what they call the "thunderers." In one such legend, a young man falls into a ravine, breaks his leg, and is subsequently deserted by his friends. He awakens to find four men dressed in cloudlike robes. When he asks them who they are, they say they are the thunderers who live in the sky and that they are there to protect him. Similarly, one Chippewa legend describes the *Gin Guin*, the "earth-rumblers" or "wheels-that-rumble-the-earth." In this narrative, a rotating wheel with lightning emanating from it descends to Earth. Once landed, Bococitti, the "fair-haired god who comes from the sky," steps out of the wheel (craft?) and walks among the people. The Algonquin tell a similar story of a great willow basket containing 12 beautiful women that also descends from the sky.

The Pawnee still relate a legend about a man named Pahokatawa who comes to Earth as a meteor. When he is killed and devoured by wild animals, the gods come from the sky and bring him back to life. He then tells the tribe that whenever they see stars falling, it is him returning to Earth. And in another example, the Snoqualmie people tell a legend of two sisters who wish that two stars in the night sky were their husbands; when they awaken in the sky world, they find that the stars are men. The older sister bears an infant named Star Child; when she takes him home to Earth, the people call him the "transformer" because he uses his heavenly powers to change—transform—the world.

PLACES OF POWER: LOCALES, STRUCTURES, AND NATURAL FORMATIONS

SUBTERRANEAN WORLDS

A belief in subterranean worlds has also been handed down in myth or legend among generations of indigenous people in the Americas. In the 1940s, the remains of 600 ancient structures were discovered near Point Hope, Alaska. The Ipiutak Ruins were laid out in a city-like grid and showed evidence that the prehistoric inhabitants possessed mathematics and cosmic knowledge comparable to that of the ancient Maya. This discovery did not surprise the local Inupiat population; they believed the discovery proved the validity of their ancient stories that told of Star People who visited and inhabited the land, and built cities both above and below ground. Even today, many Alaska natives contend that modern Alaska is the site of many underground cities built by Star People who travel back and forth between the stars and Earth. One Yupik elder related to this author how starships brought his people to Earth. The area in question (present-day Alaska and Siberia) was most similar their home planet, which was also covered with ice and snow.

In Peru, a mysterious door-like structure in the Hayu Marca mountain region near Lake Titicaca, an hour's drive from the city of Puno, has long been revered by the local indigenous people as the "city of the gods." They tell an ancient legend about a gateway to the lands of the gods. It is said that when the Spanish Conquistadors arrived in Peru and looted gold and precious stones from the Inca tribes, Amaru Meru, an Incan priest, fled the temple with a sacred golden disk and hid in the mountains of Hayu Marca. He eventually arrived at the gateway, which was being watched over by several shaman. A ceremony was performed, and, at the end, he used the golden disk to open the portal. According to the legend, a blue light emanated from a tunnel inside. Amaru Meru handed the golden disk to the shaman and then passed through the portal, never to be seen again. Even today, a small, hand-sized circular depression on the right-hand side of the entryway can be observed. The portal is guarded by 25 shaman who live in the area and permanently watch over the gateway.

The Tula Indians of Tanico considered themselves to be the "Keepers of Manataka," a spiritual mountain located in present-day Arkansas and thought to be a place where Star People once visited. According to the natives of this region, at one time there was a mountain with a cave there, but it was leveled by the state as the site was developed. This mountain was considered to be a sacred site by the Caddo, Quapaw, Osage, Tunica, and Pawnee Indians. The Tula believed that there were seven crystal caves inside the Manataka Mountain, the central one of which featured a magnificent shining crystal encoded with messages from the Star People. Likewise, Blanca Massif in the San Luis Valley of Colorado is regarded as the "sacred mountain of the east" by most Southwestern tribes, particularly the Navajo, who say that Star People arrived there in flying seed pods.

THE NAZCA LINES

The ancient Nazca culture of southern Peru is perhaps best-known for the mysterious lines and geoglyphs its members inscribed on the high desert plain in the region of Nazca. These imposing lines, which extend for hundreds of meters and depict massive images of birds, spiders, monkeys, fish, and other natural forms, are best seen from the air. Erich von Däniken proposes that the lines of Nazca were once landing strips for alien astronauts, and that the geoglyphs were markers for the space gods. While highly controversial and contested, the theory has served one purpose: It has brought the Nazca culture to the attention of the world. Maria Reiche, who has studied the Nazca markings for more than 30 years, believes that the straight lines indicated the rising or setting points of various heavenly bodies such as various constellations, the sun, and moon, and that the geoglyphs are simply impressions of various stars.

MAYAN STRUCTURES

In Uxmal, Mexico, one of the most significant ancient cities of the Maya, legend tells of a dwarf who built the ancient pyramid there overnight, a task he accomplished with the help of beings in flying machines. As the legend goes, the pyramid, a unique design in the Maya world, was built when the ruler of Uzmal challenged the dwarf to this task. If he could accomplish it in one night, the ruler said, he would relinquish his power over Uzmal to the dwarf. And so, according to the legend, he did.

NATIVE UFO ENCOUNTERS

With the new interpretations of ancient sites in the Americas and throughout the world, indigenous connections to the stars have surfaced among several other tribes. Among the most well-known of these is the Hopi and its emergence myth, which details the destruction of three earlier worlds, when wars were fought with "flying shields" propelled by some unidentified source of power. It was not until 1955 that these sorts of apocalyptic UFO themes took hold among the Hopi. The prime movers in these prophetic proclamations were a group of traditionalists who became famous both within and outside the tribe.

In 1969, when the Eagle landed on the moon, a Hopi elder told Robert Clemmer, a well-known researcher who studied Hopi prophecy, that "Hopis have been [on the moon] before. If they look around up there, they will find our rock writings" (Clemmer, 1995). Jose Lucero, a Tewa elder from the Santa Clara Pueblo, told author Nancy Red Star, "They say they get abducted [referencing alien abduction]. We get visited." (Red Star, 2000). Moreover, in 1970 Chief Dan Katchongva, a Hopi elder, announced a UFO connection to the Hopi religion. The elder Hopi told of a future when space travelers from other planets would lift the tribe's faithful on a day of purification and take them to safer worlds in the universe. According to Katchongva, an ancient rock carving near Mishongnovi, Arizona, depicting a dome-shaped, saucer-like object and a Hopi female, is the core of Hopi religious beliefs.

Ben Black Elk, the great Lakota spiritual leader, himself encountered UFOs and communicated telepathically with them; by admitting to this, of course, he completely disregarded the literalness and limited intellectual power of scientific materialism. Once, he claimed, while he was in a sweat lodge, UFOs hovered over the lodge, much to the consternation of his family, who watched the event. During his ceremonial prayers, a rock then flew into the lodge and landed between his feet. Black Elk carried this rock with him throughout his life. As well, he often referred to his sacred pipe as a means of communicating with "the ancestors in the sky."

ANCIENT MAYA AND UFOs

Theories regarding UFOs and the ancient Maya have thrived in the last decade especially. Fueled in no small part by the Maya calendar, the supposed UFO influence over ancient Maya culture often makes an appearance in discussions of this ancient civilization. The ancient Maya themselves documented interactions with Gods from the sky, in their oral traditions.

In 1776 Ramon de Ordonez y Aguiar wrote *A History of the Creation of Heaven and Earth*. The padre attempted to explain the existence of the ancient Maya city, Palenque, in the state of Chiapas, Mexico, suggesting that a race of people appeared out of the Atlantic, guided by a distinguished leader named Votan. Another account reported that Votan traveled from a distant place called Valum Chivum, a "star place," to Earth and built a tower. Beneath that tower was a place, a conduit, that allowed him to travel back and forth between the two planets.

Erich von Däniken claims that Pakal, who reigned 68 years over the ancient city, was an ancient astronaut. Reproducing a drawing of a sarcophagus lid, he compars Pakal's pose to that of Project Mercury astronauts in the 1960s, interpreting the drawings underneath him as rockets and offering it as evidence of an extraterrestrial influence on the ancient Maya city. According to von Däniken, the sarcophagus represents a seated ancient astronaut ascending to the stars in a spaceship, despite the fact that the Maya identified it as portrait of the ruler himself with the World Tree of Maya mythology.

In Palenque, Mexico, a Lacandón Maya known only as Bol revealed to this author information about invisible men from the sky who visited the Maya, and spoke of a star map that the Maya possessed that guided them to planet Earth. The Lacandón Maya, who refer to themselves as the *Hach Winik* ("true people"), live in the rain forest of Chiapas, Mexico. They are the descendants of Maya-speaking refugees who escaped assimilation and extermination during the Spanish conquest, and have maintained their traditional way of life and stories ever since. Located in the highlands of the Chiapas, Toniná, an ancient site located about 40 miles from Palenque, was often referred to as the "place of the celestial captives" by the ancient Maya. A number of local stories abound about shape-shifting sky travelers and underground alien bases around the city of Toniná.

The Zapotec, an indigenous people in the state of Oaxaca, Mexico, say that their people emerged from caves in the earth. They believe their ancestors were rocks, trees, or jaguars that were turned into people. The elite ruling class was said to have descended from supernatural beings who lived among the clouds; upon death, the rulers returned to the clouds and assumed their status as supernatural beings. The Zapotec call themselves the *Be'ena' Za'a*, which, translated, means "cloud people."

Teotitlan de Valle, a small village located about 25 miles from Oaxaca City in the foothills of the Sierra Juárez mountains, was founded by the Zapotecs around 465 BCE. It was originally named Xaquija, which means "celestial constellation" in the Zapotec language; in the Náhuatl language, Teotitian de Valle was known as the "place of the gods." In the 16th century, a Spanish friar named Juan de Cordoya recorded a legend in *The Catholic Encyclopedia* that reportedly occurred in 34 CE in Teotitlan de Valle. According to the legend, a huge bright light came out of the northern sky. It glowed for four days and then descended to a rock in the center of the village. From the light there came a great, powerful being who stood on top of the rock and glowed like the sun. He stood there for the whole village to see, glowing both day and night and lighting up the entire village. When he spoke, his voice was like thunder that boomed across the valley. In the Tiacolula valley in the state of Oaxaca, Mexico, just off Highway 190, stands the remains of Lambityeco, a small Zapotec archaeological site. The locals describe a Sky Lord who came to the village on a beam of light and built the ancient city. He married an earth woman and had a child. When his son was old enough to assume the leadership of the city, the Sky Lord left Earth on a beam of light.

In the ancient city of Quiriguá, Guatemala, the elders in the nearby village maintain that the city has always been associated with sky beings, and, in fact, that all the rulers of the ancient city were members of the "sky dynasty." An examination of the history of the site revealed that Cauac Sky, who was the first ruler of the city, was also known as Fire Burning Sky Lightning God. After Cauac, there was Sky Xul, and then Sky Imx Dog, Scroll Sky, and Jade Sky.

An ancient village named Xunantunich, located about 80 miles west of Belize City, is the site of a reappearing stone woman. The local villagers say she has been appearing at the site since 1892. The woman is dressed completely in white and has fiery red glowing eyes. She generally appears in front of El Castillo, ascends the stone stairs, and disappears into a stone wall. A local shaman maintains that the woman has the ability to cast spells upon those who see her, and that he has seen her ascend the stairs and travel on a beam of light into the sky. When this occurs, more often than not, a UFO is also observed.

Throughout Belize, Honduras, Guatemala, and Mexico, stories of encounters with Star People, Sky Gods, and ancestors from other planets abound. Many of the ancient and original stories have maintained their fidelity through the generations, without contemporary interpretations. Perhaps herein lies the real connection among indigenous peoples, Star People, and UFOs. Researchers have, by and large, ignored narratives and legends of traditional people; only in recent years have some of these ancient stories and contemporary encounters been revealed. Clearly, much still remains to be learned.

ORBS AND STAR PEOPLE

Indigenous peoples throughout the world are familiar with the phenomenon of radiant orbs, some of which are thought to transform into Star People. The Shuar, members of the Jivaroan people, an indigenous Amazonian tribe living in the mountainous region at the headwaters of the Marañón River of Ecuador, tell of being visited by luminous white or blue spheres, which they call their ancestors. The tribe does not distinguish among UFOs, ancestors, and Star People; to them, they are all one and the same. The Maya in Honduras speak of the orbs that visit the ancient site of Copan. These orbs are said to have the ability to morph into humanlike entities. In a 2004 interview conducted by this author, Xiu, an elder who lived in one of the Chorti villages that cling to the mountainsides outside Copán Ruinas, referred to them as "the ancestors with the ability to shape-shift."

ENCOUNTERS WITH STAR PEOPLE AROUND THE WORLD

AFRICA

Such star myths are not confined to indigenous peoples of North America, of course. According to certain African myths, Star People arrived in magical sky boats. The great Zulu warrior-king Shaka was said to have been kidnapped by the *mantindane* ("gray beings") and received extraordinary powers from his alien abductors. In his book *The Sirius Mystery*, Robert Temple discusses the myths of the Dogon tribesmen, an indigenous tribe who occupy a region in Mali, south of the Sahara Desert in Africa, and demonstrate amazing astronomical knowledge. The Dogon legends relate stories about Jupiter's four moons, Saturn's rings, and other celestial bodies—information unknown to scientists until recently. The Dogon say their astronomical knowledge was given to them by the *Nommos*, amphibious beings sent to Earth from Sirius for the benefit of humanity.

NORTHERN EUROPE

The Sami, the indigenous people of northern Europe who live in Sweden, Norway, Finland, and the Kola Peninsula of Russia, also have strong connections to the heavens. In the Sami conception of the world, there are three spheres: the heavenly, the earthly, and the infernal regions. Gods and godly creatures inhabit all three. Their *noajdde*, or shamans, travel from the earthly realm to the other two worlds to speak with the gods and deceased ancestors.

AUSTRALIA

Australian Aborigines have their myths of the *Wandjinas*, the supreme spirit beings and creators of the land and all people. The Worora, the Ngarinyin, and the Wunumbul are the three living Wandjina (also spelled Wondjina) tribes and custodians of the oldest known figurative art in Australia. This art, painted on rocks and in caves, represents the Wandjinas with white faces, large, black eyes, no mouths, and heads surrounded by halos. The ancient paintings have been interpreted as representations of ancient astronauts, suggesting that extraterrestrials visited Earth and had direct contact with the Aboriginals, and perhaps even played a role in their creation, as reflected in their "Dreamtime" stories. According to the Aborigines, the creators were powerful beings that had the ability to shape-shift, and ascended into the heavens to meet with Sky Gods who bore such names as Bundjil, Balame, Biral, and Goin.

EASTER ISLAND

Rapa Nui (Easter Island) is best known for its 900 immense stone statues, called *Moai*, scattered across the island. The indigenous islanders have a legend that the statues were moved to their platforms and raised upright by the use of *mana*, or mind power. According to legend, the god Makemake commanded them to walk or to float through the air, and, according to one legend, use was made of a finely crafted stone sphere, 2 1/2 feet in diameter, called *te pito kura* (meaning "the golden navel" or "the navel of light"), to focus the *mana*. Erich von Däniken suggests that extraterrestrials stranded on the island built the *Moai* to serve as beacons to other star travelers. As if this suggestion were not outrageous enough, he adds that the extraterrestrials built these structures in order to memorialize their arrival on the island and to ensure that the indigenous people would not forget about this important aspect of their history.

NEW ZEALAND

The chief spiritual elder of the Māori, the indigenous people of Aotearoa (New Zealand), Mac Wiremu Ruka, speaking at the Star Knowledge Conference in South Dakota, said that the Māori came to Earth from the stars. The Māori connection to the heavens is obvious in their mythology. The Māori conception of the heavens (Sky Father) consists of several discrete layers: Rangi (heaven closest to earth), Ranguinui (great heavens), Rangiroa (expansive heavens), Te Ranginui-e-tū-nei (the great-standing heavens), Te Rangiātea (the great breadth of the heavens), and Te Rangitiketike and Te Rangipāmamao (which denote loftiness and remoteness). The names Te Rangiwhakataka and Te Rangitakataka actually describe how the heavens reached down to the horizon to meet Papatūānuku, the Earth Mother. Thus, the Sky Father and Earth Mother joined together to create the Māori.

CONCLUSION: AN INDIGENOUS PERSPECTIVE

During the course of my research, I walked among indigenous peoples of the world, shared their meals, joined in family gatherings, participated in traditional ceremonies, engaged in events of both merriment and misfortune, celebrated births and mourned the deceased, and listened to stories, both ancient and contemporary, about Sky Gods, Star People, and UFOs. During my journey, I became convinced that the AAT (ancient alien theory) was not only offensive to the indigenous cultures of the world, but it was downright wrong.

The fact is that there is no real evidence to support the theory, only an assumption based upon an underlying premise that indigenous peoples did not have the intelligence or capability to create their ancient cities and monuments. What is even more evident is the implication that indigenous cultures could not possibly have been equal to, let alone superior to Western civilization in that regard. In other words, if Western cultures could not build such cities, nobody on Earth could; it *had* to have been an alien race.

One university-educated Maya historian I spoke with, known only as Cocom, said it best:

Von Däniken never asked us what we thought of his theories. If he had, perhaps we might have told him the truth. But then, it does no good to talk to white men. They believe themselves to be superior to the dark-skin [sic] man and they write the books. Many of our elders say we are the Star People, and our connection varies from one subgroup to another. I believe we are descendants of the Star People, who built these magnificent cites, but our old stories tell of a great cataclysm that visited our world and it destroyed people, land, crops, and even our great spiritual leaders. So what happens when everything familiar is gone? You do what any people would do. You survive. But at the same time, you lose faith in the old ways and you build a new one. The only thing that matters is how to survive and take care of your family. That is the story of the Maya. We have been surviving ever since we arrived on planet

Earth. We have survived invasions, wars, hurricanes, meteors, and volcanoes. We survived the invaders. We will survive the white man's theories. The important thing is, we know who we are. I don't believe the invaders ever knew who they were, nor do their descendants today.

My rejection of the AAT does *not* mean that I do not believe that Star People ever visited Mother Earth; I do. Whereas most anthropologists discard Native legends and stories of so-called primitive people as stories borne of superstitious cultures, this author, like Deloria, believes that something happened to cause these legends to come into being. In fact, I believe that the history of our Mother Earth and that of our progenitors have been faithfully recorded in legend, myth, and lore, and that, ergo, indigenous peoples have a special connection to the stars.

I am also convinced that Star People continue to visit our planet. Originally, it appeared as though the visitors were our ancestors, as so many of the ancient and contemporary stories reveal. More recent stories indicate that universe is becoming ever smaller, and that other entities that have no previous connection with Earth or its people are visiting our planet. Several of the stories I heard spoke of such events and brought warnings along with them. For example, Xun Péres, a Guatemalan Maya elder, said to me:

> Our elders taught us that the people from the stars came to Earth and stayed. They did not leave, as some of the white men write. But catastrophe struck the great civilizations. We are what remain. We are the survivors. But be warned: all great civilizations collapse, whether through war, famine, a weather event, or invasion. They all meet their end, and the next civilization 5,000 years from now may unearth the Statue of Liberty, and speculate that she was the goddess of flame who brought fire to the world. I have seen your Statue of

Liberty. I went to New York to the United Nations. You have many gods in New York City that the people will cling to if their world is destroyed, but, like the Maya, the survivors will choose not to remember. So do not be dismayed by our silence. We keep the truth close to our heart. The invaders were never interested in the truth because they believed themselves superior.... Now they look to us for answers, but they are not to be revealed to those who call themselves experts and benefit from our stories financially.

There is no question that many forgotten civilizations have preceded us whose attainments were terminated by cataclysmic or man-made events. It may be that humanity's origins and history lie in the oral traditions of indigenous people; it may be that we are *all* space travelers.

In Vine Deloria's book *Evolution, Creationism, and Other Modern Myths*, the Ogallala scholar presents the premise that science in general assumes superiority of thought over the collective memory of people. The authority of truth that was once invested in traditional wisdom was cast aside by the scientific community, which regarded this wisdom as mere myth and legend. If the evidence could not be explained scientifically, it was discarded. Today, as we struggle with the challenges of the modern world, I believe there are valuable solutions in the ancient accounts of indigenous peoples. Significant scientific discoveries in various fields seem to demonstrate there is a connection between the modern world and ancient knowledge. Crossing many fields of study, this combination of science and ancient knowledge paves the way for a new kind of awareness about our reality and who we are as humans. But to access this knowledge and to accept it, would mean that these ancient indigenous cultures and their descendants had superior knowledge. At the time of this writing, Western cultures have by and large been unable to concede this fact.

As I interviewed indigenous people who had personal encounters with UFOs and Star People, I learned of their ancient stories as well as their personal encounters. I listened to their mysterious, mystical, spiritual experiences and otherworldly encounters, and did not ask for evidence. Their testimony was all I needed to believe in their trustworthiness; I made no assumptions and drew no conclusions. Along the way, I learned other secrets, too, secrets that indigenous people know but keep private. They cannot be revealed here. As I ponder those secrets that lie buried in the collective knowledge of indigenous peoples and are passed from one generation to another, I am reminded of something Rigoberta Menchú, Guatemalan K'iche' Maya activist and Nobel Peace Prize recipient, wrote: "I'm still keeping my Indian identity a secret. I'm still keeping what I think no one should know. Not even anthropologists or intellectuals, no matter how many books they have, can find out all our secrets" (from his book *I, Rigoberta Menchú*). Those secrets have been handed down for countless generations and define these people *as* indigenous. Those secrets they are not willing to share, nor am I.

Bibliography/Sources

Agrest, Matest M. "The Historical Evidence of Paleocontacts." *Ancient Skies, Volume 20, Number 6*. Highland Park, Ill.: Ancient Astronaut Society. pp. 1–3.

Arbachakov, Alexander, and Luba Arbachakov. *The Last of the Shor Shaman*. Blue Ridge Summit, Penn.: Moon Books, 2008.

Bauval, Robert, and Adrian Gilbert. *The Orion Mystery*. Toronto: Doubleday Canada, 1996.

Bennett, Colin. *Politics of the Imagination: The Life, Work and Ideas of Charles Fort*. London: Head Press, 2002.

Best, Elsdon. *The Astronomical Knowledge of the Māori Genuine and Empirical*. New Haven, Conn.: Kiwi Publishers, 2002 .

Bierhorst, John (ed.). *The Monkey's Haircut and Other Stories Told by the Maya.* New York: William Morrow, 1986.

Black Elk, Wallace, and William S. Lyon. *Black Elk: The Sacred Ways of the Lakota.* New York: HarperOne, 2003.

"Blue People": *www.burlingtonnews.net/bluepeople.*

Boremanse, Didier. *Contes et mythologie des indiens lacandons.* L'Harmattan, 1986.

Carlson, John. B. "America's Ancient Skywatchers." *National Geographic,* Vol. 177, No. 3 March 1990: 76–107.

Castner, James, L. *Native Peoples.* Marshall Cavendish, 2002.

"The Case of the Ancient Astronauts." *Horizon,* August 3, 1978.

The Catholic Encyclopedia. Robert Appleton Company, 1912.

Cazeau, Charles J., and Stuart D. Scott, Jr. *Exploring the Unknown: Great Mysteries Reexamined.* Cambridge, Mass.: Da Capo Press, 1980.

Clark, Ella E., and Margo Edmonds. *Voices of the Winds: Native American Legends.* Castle Books, 2003.

Clark, Jerome. *The UFO Encyclopedia.* Omnigraphics, 1988.

———. "The Extraterrestrial Hypothesis in the Early UFO Age" *UFOs and Abductions: Challenging the Borders of Knowledge.* David M. Jacobs, editor; University Press of Kansas, 2000 (pp. 122–140).

Clemmer, Richard O. "Then You Will Rise and Strike My Head From My Neck: Hopi Prophecy and the Discourse of Empowerment." *American Indian Quarterly* 19:31–73, 1995.

Collyns, Robin. *Did Spacemen Colonize the Earth?* Washington, D.C.: Regnery, 1976.

Cowan, James. *Messengers of the Gods: Tribal Elders Reveal the Ancient Wisdom of the Earth.* New York: Harmony, 1993.

Curran Douglas. *In Advance of the Landing: Folk Concepts of Outer Space.* New York: Abbeville Press, 1985.

Deloria, Vine, Jr. *Evolution, Creationism, and Other Modern Myths: A Critical Inquiry.* Golden, Colo.: Fulcrum Publishing, 2002.

————. *God Is Red.* Golden, Colo.: Fulcrum Publishing. 30th Anniversary Edition, 2003.

Elkin, A.P. *Aboriginal Men of High Degree: Initiation and Sorcery in the World's Oldest Tradition.* Rochester, Vt.: Inner Traditions, 1993.

Erdoes, Richard, and Alfonso Ortiz. *American Indian Myths and Legends.* New York: Pantheon Books, 1984.

Fort, Charles. *The Book of the Damned.* New York: Cosimo Classics, 2004.

Gamboa, Pedro Sarmiento De. "Viracocha and the Coming of the Incas." *History of the Incas,* translated by Clements Markham, The Hakluyt Society, 1907.

Gibbons, Gavin. *They Rode in Space Ships.* New York: Citadel Press, 1957.

Hamilton III, William F. *Cosmic Top Secret: America's Secret UFO Program.* Atlanta, Ga.: Inner Light Publications,1991.

Hancock, Graham. *Fingerprints of the Gods.* New York: Three Rivers Press, 1996.

Harner, Michael J. *Jivaro: People of the Sacred Waterfalls.* University of California Press, 1984.

————. *The Way of the Shaman.* New York: Harper and Row, 1980.

Harris, Christie. *Sky Man on the Totem Pole?* New York: Atheneum, 1975.

Hawking, Steven. "Humans Should Fear Aliens." *www.huffingtonpost.com/2010/04/25/stephen-hawking-aliens_n_551035.html#s84595&title=Charlie_Rose\.*

Holroyd, Stuart. *Alien Intelligence.* London: David and Charles, 1979.

Jamieson, Sue and John E. Mack. "Shamanic Journeys and UFO Encounters: A Consideration of Two Avenues to an Expanded Reality." *Journal of the Foundation for Shamanic Studies*, Spring/Summer 2003, Vol. 16, No. 1.

Jefferson, Thomas, and Benjamin Smith Barton. *New Views of the Origin of the Tribes and Nations of America.* Ulan Press, 2011 (previously published in 1798).

Jennings, Jack A. "Impact of Contact on Religion." *Second Look* (January–February): 11–14, 41, 1980.

Jessup, M.K. *The Case for the UFO: Unidentified Flying Objects.* New York: Bantam Books, 1955.

Kalweit, Holger. *Dreamtime and Inner Space.* Shambhala Press, 1988.

Krupp, Edward C. *Echoes of the Ancient Skies: The Astronomy of Lost Civilisations.* Oxford: Oxford University Press, 1983: 153.

Lewis, James R., editor. *UFOs and Popular Culture.* Santa Barbara, Calif.: ABC-CLIO, Inc., 2000.

Mack, John E. *Passport to the Cosmos: Human Transformation and Alien Encounters.* New York: Crown Publishers, 1999.

Mackenzie, Donald A. *Pre-Columbian America: Myths and Legends.* Senate, 1996.

Marshall, James Vance. *Stories From the Billabong.* Frances Lincoln Books, 2010.

Menchu, Rigoberta. *I, Rigoberta Menchu.* Ed. Elisabeth Burgos-Debray. Trans. Ann Wright. London: Verso, 1984, p. 24.

Miller, Mary, and Karl Taube. *The Gods and Symbols of Ancient Mexico and the Maya: An Illustrated Dictionary of Mesoamerican Religion.* New York: Thames and Hudson, 1993.

Mills, Kenneth R. *Colonial Spanish America: a Documentary History.* Lanham, Md.: Rowman & Littlefield, 1998.

Moseley, James W., and Karl T. Pflock. *Shockingly Close to the Truth.* Amherst, N.Y.: Prometheus Books, 2002.

Narby, Jeremy. *The Cosmic Serpent: DNA and the Origins of Knowledge.* New York: Putnam, 1998.

Neihardt, John G. *Black Elk Speaks: Being the Life Story of a Holy Man of the Oglala Sioux.* The Premier Edition, State University of New York Press, 2008.

Nicholson, Irene. *Mexican and Central American Mythology.* London: Paul Hamlyn, 1967.

Oberg, J. E. "Astronauts and UFOs: The Whole Story." *Spaceworld* N-2–158 (February): 4–28, 1977.

Olcott, William Tyler. *Star Lore: Myths, Legends, and Facts.* 1911 Dover, 2004.

Olien, Michael D. "Did Ancient Astronauts Bring Civilization?" *The Human Myth: An Introduction to Anthropology.* New York: Harper & Row,1978.

Orbell, Margaret. *The Natural World of the Maori.* Christchurch, New Zealand: Canterbury University Press,1996.

———. *A Concise Encyclopedia of Māori Myth and Legend.* Christchurch, New Zealand: Canterbury University Press, 1998.

Orser, Charles E. *Race and Practice in Archaeological Interpretation.* University of Pennsylvania Press, 2003.

Pauwels, Louis, and Jacques Bergier. *The Morning of the Magicians: Secret Societies, Conspiracies, and Vanished Civilizations.* Rochester, Vt.: Destiny Books, 2008.

Persinger, M.A. "What Factors Can Account for UFO Experiences?" *IUR* 3, no. 10–11 (October–November): 21, 1978.

Persinger, M.A., and G.F. Lafrenière. *Space Time Transients and Unusual Events.* Chicago, Ill.: Nelson Hall, 1977.

Peters, Ted. "Heavenly Chariots and Flying Saucers. " In *MUFON 1976 UFO Symposium Proceedings: New Frontiers in UFO Research.* ed. N. Joseph Gurney and Walter H. Andrus Jr., 53–64. Seguin, Tex.: Mutual UFO Network.

Peterson, Scott. *Native American Prophecies: Examining the History, Wisdom and Startling Predictions of Visionary Native Americans.* New York: Paragon House, 1990.

Randle, Kevin D. "Does Pop Culture Affect Our Views?" In *MUFON 1996 International UFO Symposium Proceedings: Ufology: A Scientific Enigma.* Ed. Walter H. Andrus Jr., 17–25. Seguin, Tex.: Mutual UFO Network.

Read, Kay Almere and Jason J. Gonzalez. *Mesoamerican Mythology. A Guide to the Gods, Heroes, Rituals, and Beliefs of Mexico and Central America.* Oxford, 2002.

Red Star, Nancy. *Star Ancestors: Indian Wisdom Keepers share the Teachings of the Extraterrestrials.* Rochester, Vt.: Destiny Books, 2000.

Reed, A.W. *Aboriginal Myths, Legends, and Fables.* London: New Holland Publishers; New edition, 1999.

———. *Reed book of Māori mythology.* Self-published, 2004.

Richie, David. *UFO: The Definitive Guide to Unidentified Flying Objects and Related Phenomena.* New York: Facts on File, 1994.

Roberts, Llyn. "Shaman From the Stars." *Earth Star Magazine*, 2002.

Roth, Christopher F. "Ufology as Anthropology: Race, Extraterrestrials, and the Occult" In *E.T. Culture: Anthropology in Outerspaces.* Ed. Debbora Battaglia. Durham, N.C.: Duke University Press, 2005.

Roys, Ralph. *The Book of Chilam Balam of Chumayel.* University of Oklahoma Press, 2012.

Rubenstein, Steven. *Alejandro Tsakimp: A Shuar Healer in the Margins of History.* University of Nebraska Press, 2002.

Sagan, Carl. "Night Walkers and Mystery Mongers: Sense and Nonsense at the Edge of Science." *Broca's Brain*. New York: Random House, 1979.

Shapiro, Joshua. "Star Knowledge UFO Conference Update." *Contact Forum* 4, no. 5 (September–October): p. 8–9, 1996.

Shklovski, I.S., and Carl Sagan. *Intelligent Life in the Universe*. Holden-Day, 1966.

Sitchin, Zechariah. *The Twelfth Planet*. New York: Avon Books, 1976.

———. *The Wars of Gods and Men*. New York: Avon Books, 1985.

———. *Genesis Revisited: Is Modern Science Catching Up with Ancient Knowledge?* New York: Avon Books, 1990.

———. *When Time Began: The First New Age*. New York: Avon Books, 1993.

———. *Divine Encounters: A Guide to Visions, Angels, and Other Emissaries*. Avon Books, 1995.

Smith, Ramsay W. *Myths and Legends of the Australian Aborigines*. Mineola, N.Y.: Dover Publications, 2003.

Somé, Malidoma Patrice. *Of Water and the Spirit: Ritual Magic, and Initiation in the Life of an African Shaman*. London: Penguin Arkana, 1994.

Standing Elk. "Rods on the Yankton." *Contact Forum* 5, no. 3 (May/June): p. 22–23, 1997.

Story Ronald. *Guardians of the Universe?* New York: St. Martin's Press, 1980.

Taube, Karl. *The Major Gods of Ancient Yucatan*. Dumbarton Oaks, 1992.

———. *Aztec and Maya Myths*. British Museum, 1993.

Tedlock, Dennis. *Popol Vuh*. New York: Simon and Schuster, 2007.

Temple, Robert. *The Sirius Mystery*. New York: St. Martin's Press, 1976.

Thompson, J. Eric S. *Maya History and Religion. Civilization of the American Indian Series.* No. 99, University of Oklahoma Press, 1970.

Thompson, Keith. *Angels and Aliens: UFOs and the Mythic Imagination.* Boston, Mass.: Addison-Wesley Publishing, 1991.

Trench, Brinsley Le Poer. *Mysterious Visitors: The UFO Story.* New York: Stein and Day Publishers, 1971.

Trench, Brinsley Le Poer. *The Sky People.* Clarksburg, W. Va.: Saucerian Books; 1st edition, 1960.

Vallée, Jacques. *Passport to Magonia: From Folklore to Flying Saucers.* Washington, D.C.: Regnery, 1969.

Van Cleef, Jabez. *God Wears Many Skins: Myth and Folklore of the Sami People.* Create Space Independent Publishing Platform, 2008.

Von Däniken, Erich. *Chariots of the Gods? Unsolved Mysteries of the Past.* New York: Bantam Books, 1968.

Ywahoo, Dhyani. *Voices of Our Ancestors: Cherokee Teachings from the Wisdom Fire.* Boston, Mass.: Shambhala Press, 1987.

THE LOST ARMIES OF CAMBYSES

BY JOHN RICHARD WARD AND SCOTT ALAN ROBERTS

A man of true caliber is one who combines fear when laying his plans, so that he weighs up everything that might happen to him, with courage in carrying out those plans.

—Herodotus, *The Histories*, Book 7.49

There was an age, in the ancient worlds of old, when gods walked among men on the Earth. It was a time when mankind emerged from the shadows of the cave, casting off the final vestiges of the paradisal garden to set out into the rough world to flourish, clad only in his ingenuity inspired by gifts bestowed by the pantheon of his gods: writing, mathematics, geometry, and the ability to harness the land, enabling him to provide shelter, security, and sustenance for himself, his family, and his fellow man. It was a time of exponential growth and prosperity, when mud and stone evolved into great monumental edifices that rose far above the ground, reaching toward the heavens in gratitude for the great offerings conferred. But it was also a time of conquest, pillage, and rape, for as these gifts grew and took root with the emerging civilizations, so also man waxed weary of his own lot, and in turn, looked to his neighbor with envious eyes, coveting the bounty the other had harvested. From these humble beginnings emerged the great empires, the "anthropology in a nutshell" that fills our dusty old school books, rife with tales of kings, queens, armies, and leaders of men; lovers and poets, philosophers and magicians, oracles and prophets, all becoming gods in their own right. The fodder of the fire of mankind; the very sustenance of myth, legend, and tales of heroic deeds echoing throughout the labyrinth of human history, burned in the peoples of antiquity: Greeks, Romans, Persians, Spartans, Egyptians, Libyans, Sea Peoples, and Hysko— the list as endless as the tablets, inscriptions, scrolls, and pages that record their accomplishments.

191

The history of civilization is synonymous with the history of war. Triumph after triumph, the battles never ending, enumerated conquests continued unabated as man sought to increase his empire, wielding imposed power and fragile authority far beyond the controlling confines of his own homeland. Boundaries were endlessly shifting to and fro, and enslavement of common people and abolishment of native gods and goddesses went hand-in-hand with the victories. New deities emerged from faraway lands, imposed upon the indigenous, now conquered and impoverished people. Political corruption and intrigue, combined with diplomatically arranged marriages between the ruling classes of the various nations, were now becoming commonplace. Tribute, gifts, and dowries established a delicate status quo among the rulers of the known world. Even within the comfort of their own ruling families, incestuous alliances between siblings established a façade of stability that belied the growing mistrust between them. From what should have been natural family loyalties, the overflowing chalice of power and wealth captured the overzealous imaginations and desires of the jealous sons of kings, discarding the natural for the perceived.

These uneasy, artificially imposed alliances did not stop the increasing yearning for power, nor did it abate the thirst for blood, gore, and spoils of war—the lust of conscribed, amassed armies. Schisms developed within the various homelands, bringing parricide, conspiracies, invasions, war, famine, poverty, and death to those who were enslaved. The people became pawns in the struggle for land and dominion. Yet, emerging from within the whirlwind of wielded power of the empire-builders was the tenacious determination to exert one's own individuality. Man had learned to write and record his history, but with it came the responsibility of preserving knowledge and wisdom; in so doing, he created education, a pursuit that was no longer preserved for the higher classes and those who dwelled within the sacred confines of the temple. These semi-educated people began to develop individual characteristics, languages, religions, and cultural identities separating them from their neighbors. One such people were the Dorians, from the ethnic group of the early Greeks, which included the Aeolians, Achaeans, and the Ionians. Like their counterparts, they spread across the southern boundaries of what was to become the coastlines of Europe. Halikarnassos, a small fishing village on the northeastern shores of the Mediterranean in Asia Minor, was one such example of the expanding Dorian empire. It was here that they settled and established themselves as a thriving seaport. It was a place they could call home, assimilating the indigenous tribes of the original island of Zephyria into their newly established Dorian colony.

In 484 BCE, in this small but thriving city and strategic seaport, Herodotus, one of humanity's greatest historians, was born. Not much is known of his family or his earlier life as a child in Halikarnassos, but personal quotes of his love for the island of Samos may be an indication that he had spent some time there during the turmoil that developed throughout the tyrannical rule of Lygdamis of Naxos. His family was very possibly in some type of exile, as they were in opposition to the tyrant's authoritarian rule. It is evident that Herodotus received some sort of formal education as a child, most probably at the hands of one of the priests at the local temple, which was dedicated to one of the various Greek gods. Poseidon, Medusa, and Athena were all worshipped in the Halikarnassos of his day, along with Anthes, the son of Poseidon, which granted Halikarnassos the attributed accolade of "Antheadae." It is also quite possible that Herodotus may have received his tutelage from his astute uncle, Panyasis, spending most of his days enthralled by some tale of the great and inspiring legend of Hercules, for which Panyasis became so famous as a poet, and yet, which also led to his untimely demise at the hands of Halikarnassus's new autocratic ruler, Lygdamis of Naxos. As young men are wont to do, Herodotus probably daydreamed of

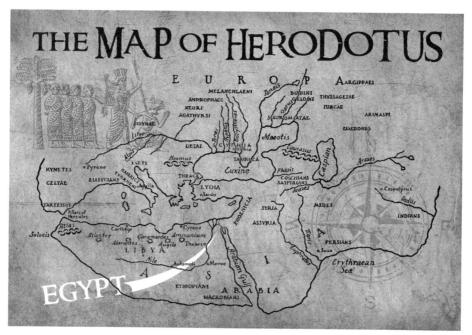

The map of the world by Herodotus, originally rendered in the 3rd century BCE. *Adaptation by Scotty Roberts,* © *2014.*

one day traveling across the great sea to explore the east and all its riches. Prompted by his uncle, Panyasis, Herodotus yearned to walk in the footsteps of the gods themselves and gaze upon the marvels of man's achievements with his own eyes, recording his own observations, personal encounters, and adventures for posterity. But his youthful aspirations met an untimely demise, as his uncle's execution more than likely was the event that forced the young Herodotus to leave his childhood far behind and flee for the shores of the newly enslaved Egypt, which had recently fallen under Persian rule.

By this time Halikarnassos had established a sea trade between the Turkish mainland and Egypt, both during and after the invasion of Egypt, by the neurotic, young Persian ruler Cambyses, the son of Cyrus the Great. It was Cambyses who ushered in a new period for Egypt, inaugurating the 27th dynasty in what is known today as the Late Period of Egypt. Cambyses felt drawn into a forced invasion of

Egypt out of honorable vengeance to the treachery of Egypt's Pharaoh Ahmose II, who deceived him by sending Nitetis, the daughter of the late Pharaoh Apries, instead of, apparently, his own beautiful daughter to wed. But by all accounts, Herodotus redacted this vengeful story within the pages of his *Histories*. It was said that a skilled but somewhat out-of-favor eye doctor had been sent to the Persian court, after the King of Kings, Cambyses, had requested an Egyptian ophthalmologist. Not wishing to cause any distrust or ill will between the two great rulers, Pharaoh Ahmose II sent one of his physicians, whom he had wished to expel from his royal court but had thus far failed to find reasonable grounds for the expulsion. The pharaonic physician's self-absorbed guilt at having to leave his beloved family behind in Egypt while he took up his new enforced office in exile with Cambyses led him to persuade his new master to request a marriage with one of Pharaoh's daughters. But in so doing, he would cause the Egyptian Pharaoh to deceive Cambyses, for in accordance with Egyptian tradition, no royal Egyptian woman would ever be presented to a non-Egyptian for marriage. At the time, the practice was simply unheard of.

So, not wishing to offend the powerful King of Persia, and in a gesture of intended good will and political harmony between the two great kingdoms—but at the same time not wishing to see his own daughter fall victim to the harem of the Persian King—Ahmose sent the young lady, Nitetis, the tall and beautiful daughter of his predecessor, Apries. After having been outfitted with the finest Egyptian wardrobe and a dowry befitting any princess, Nitetis arrived at the court of the King of Persia. The king, however, while admiring his newly arrived royal concubine, was immediately informed by her of the Pharaoh's deception, as well as her true identity as daughter to Pharaoh Apries, who had years earlier been murdered at the hands of Ahmose, during his uprising against her father Pharaoh Apries. The revolt had been led by the then-General Ahmose, who was now the Pharaoh of Egypt.

Upon hearing of such treachery and flagrant deceit by the belligerent Ahmose, Cambyses was thrown into a fit of rage, and vowed to revenge his honor and invade Egypt, taking it for his own. Unfortunately, before Cambyses had reached the sacred walls of Memphis, Pharaoh Ahmose II had already entered the sacred pillars of the underworld, his mummified body lying safely within its tomb, while his Ba (soul) enjoyed the freedom of the day. Pharaoh's son and somewhat inexperienced successor, Pharaoh Psammetichus III, had only been installed upon the throne of Egypt for six months before he was to be tested upon the battlefield of Pelusium in the spring of 525 BCE, on the eastern frontiers of Egypt.

Raging forward across the Sinai desert, raising clouds of dust and debris high up into the sun-white sky, obfuscating the rays of Ra from the men of foot as they charged onward with their spears and shields, Cambyses, driven by pure contempt for the young Pharaoh, drove his chariot across the desert floor. Ahead of his men, as only a warring, conquering monarch could do, the Persian king reined in his team of horses singlehandedly with his left arm, his body pulling backward against the pull of the leather reins wrapped tightly around his forearm. In his right hand he held aloft his battle sharpened kopis blade, his akinakes dagger sidearm rattling at his thigh. The entire thunderous cacophony of the Persian armed forces of battle-hardened veterans, along with Greek mercenaries screaming their battle cries, must have been a most fearful display of unrivaled power.

The horrified young Pharaoh stood trembling upon the deck of his chariot, cocooned in his laced Lamellar armour, his Khepresh crown bearing heavily down upon his brow, its golden Ureaus glistening in the midday sun. He was painfully aware that the very sovereignty of Egypt was in the balance, and that Maat—the Egyptian god of law, balance, and justice—had abandoned the battlefield and with it, his sole responsibility to restore order and keep chaos at bay. Beads of sweat ran down the young Pharaoh's anxious face;

not wishing to be perceived as weak by his men, he raised his gilded wrist band to his face, the heat of which evaporated the sweat—and his worries—immediately. His harnessed horses biting and frothing at their bits furiously, while his spearman and bowman stood silently but nervously behind him on the footplate of the chariot, his loyal, seasoned generals and captains looked to him for direction, guidance, and support as their living personification of Ra. But instead of strength and leadership, they saw only an inexperienced young man, who had been forced into an unwinnable scenario. The awaiting Egyptian army stood fast, their leather beaten shields held aloft, their Khopeshs, spears, and axes beating hard against the stretched animal skin shields, attempting in vain to drown out the tremendous din that approached them. The bowmen, their fingers held tight at the ready against straining bowstrings, awaited the coming order to release their volley into the ever-approaching Persian army that was gaining ground, drawing closer and closer with each heartbeat. And then, as if in a single moment, the order was given to charge, and the two armies collided and blended into a morass of brandishing blades and flailing bodies. The sands of the Sinai desert floor pooled red with the blood of the clashing humanity, creating a gorish mud at their dancing feet, the screams of terror and pain as mortal strikes of metal blades against the bare skin of the foot soldiers ripped and dismembered, scattering among them entrails and limbs. Solider after soldier fell to his death, while horses from both camps ran riderless, scared and wild, their empty embattled chariots drawn behind them as they ran through the lines of entangled and furiously fighting men. A hot knife through butter, trampling and crushing beneath their hooves the wounded, the dying, and the dead as they lay upon the bloodstained ground.

The Egyptian generals and captains looked helplessly on as the hand-to-hand battle ensued. The young Pharaoh knew he had lost his beloved Egypt to the Persian king who had been dishonored by his father. And what crime had he committed other than being the

Cambyses meets Pharaoh Psammeticus at Pelusium. Adrien Guignet (1816–1854).
Source: WikiComons: http://upload.wikimedia.org/wikipedia/commons
/5/55/Meeting_Between_Cambyses_II_and_Psammetichus_III.jpg.

son of a trickster, the heir to a loving father who wanted nothing more than to protect his own daughter from the filthy hands of a non-Egyptian? His punishment, he knew, would be far greater in the afterlife than it would be upon this lost battlefield.

When the day's battle had finally abated, the mighty Egyptian army was utterly lost, slain and sifted to the four winds. The remaining loyal soldiers and their young Pharaoh fled for the safety of the secure walls of Memphis. It was there that they would stand their ground in a lengthy, but eventually unsuccessful siege. Fifty thousand Egyptian soldiers lost their lives upon the Pelusium desert wastelands, compared to the seven thousand reportedly lost by the invading Persians.

As Pharaoh sought refuge for his family and men behind the fortified walls of Memphis, Cambyses sent forth a ship bearing a delegation to negotiate the terms of the surrender of the Egyptian king. However, upon seeing the Mytilenean ship approaching Memphis upon

Human remains scattered along the trade route in the western desert. Photo by John Ward, © 2012.

the Nile waters, the Egyptians left the protection of the walled city and took the crew captive. Despite its messengers being under the banner of Egypt's capitulation, the angry Egyptians slew everyone on board, their bodies ripped limb from limb by the uncontrollable mob. As wild dogs would a wounded lamb in the wilderness, they tore at the delegation of Cambyses, which only succeeded in fueling the infuriation and insatiable anger of the Persian monarch.

An interesting observation was recorded by Herodotus with regard to the sun-bleached skeletal remains of both the Persians and the Egyptians that had fallen to the sword that dreadful day in Egyptian history at Pelusium. It is said that the skulls of the Persians would break into pieces by the slightest touch, yet the sun-bleached skulls of the Egyptians were as hard as the granite quarries of Swenett (Aswan). By the time Herodotus arrived in Egypt, he deduced from his observation that the Egyptians, due to leaving their heads uncovered during their daily lives, allowed the blistering heat of the Egyptian sun to "harden their skulls," whereas the Persians, who kept their heads covered with felt caps throughout their lives, unwittingly reduced the thickness of their skulls, thereby producing this astounding affect.

Eventually the young, embittered Pharaoh had no choice but to surrender Egypt and all her glory into the hands of the invading Persians. Amasis, son of Psammetichus and crown Prince of Egypt, was led out of the city past his father, who, with his head bowed toward the ground, devoid of any sign of grief or sorrow, was no doubt burdened over Egypt's defeat and the end of his personal dynasty. Amasis, together with 2,000 other Egyptian prisoners, their arms tied and shackled, nooses hanging from their necks, were put to their deaths, their bodies ripped apart limb by limb and left to rot upon the desert floor in the scorching sun, a testament of revenge for the slaughtered Mytilenean crew that had approached Memphis to broker peace. The emotional test set by Cambyses to arouse the imperturbability of the fallen sovereign was unsuccessful, yet when the broken Pharaoh gazed upon the frail body of a once-noble friend who now begged in the streets for a mere morsel of food, his royal reserve finally broke. Psammetichus began to scream and weep, pulling at his hair as if he were in mourning. Upon hearing the reactions of the devastated fallen Pharaoh, Cambyses felt pity, and exiled Psammetichus to Susa, one of the main capitals of the Achaemenid Persian Empire.

Still embittered and full of anger at the dishonor dealt him by the deceitful late Pharaoh Ahmose II, Cambyses traveled from the newly captured city of Memphis to the ancient city of Zau to visit the tomb of his dead adversary, Pharaoh Ahmose II. Zau lay at the fifth nome of Lower Egypt, on the western Canopic branch of the Nile (ancient Greek Sais, modern-day Sa el Hagar), among the northern marshlands of the Delta.

Set beyond the enormous mud brick enclosure walls that surrounded the ancient city of Zau, the cultic city had stood defiant
against time itself for more than 2,000 years. Cambyses and his en-
tourage, upon entering the confines of the city, would had to have
walked along the narcissistic Ahmose's newly erected, Sphinx-lined
processional route, which led to the monumental gated pylon providing access to the primordial temple dedicated to the cult of Neith,
the Goddess of war, hunting, and wisdom. There among the tow-
ering painted columns and dressed stone cornices within the first
courtyard, devotees worshiped the many visiting Egyptian gods and
goddesses associated with the cultic temple—Osiris, Horus, Isis, and
Hathor among many others. All the worshippers scattered for the
safety of the inner chambers, as Cambyses, by his mere presence,
defiled the sanctity of this holy place. One can easily imagine Cambyses mocking the deity Neith, the Egyptian Goddess of war who
held her spears in her hand. The Persian king stood before her and
proclaimed his victory over the Egyptian army at Pelusium, due not
only to the Egyptians lack of military prowess, but in disdain for the
pathetic female goddess they worshipped and to whom they paid
homage. Far better it would have been for the Egyptians to have
worshipped a masculine deity that would have possessed the necessary qualities of warring and strength. It is no wonder that the Egyptians fell like flies upon the battlefield!

Situated within the courtyards and chambers of the temple
grounds lay the mummified remains, entombed for eternity, of the
Pharaohs of the 26th dynasty. Among the tombs of the interred
monarchs, only one particular tomb was of interest to Cambyses:
that of the last resting place of his former nemesis, the instigator
of this invasion, Pharaoh Ahmose II. And the tomb itself was indeed as royally befitted as that of any other past Pharaoh, with its
ornate palm tree pillars supporting the immense, dressed stone ceil-
ings above, decorated with blankets of stars representing the heavens

and Pharaoh's own celestial journey. Reliefs depicted colorful scenes from the Book of Earth, characterizing the journey that the sun god takes through the earth, and is associated with the deities of Osiris, Ra, and the Pharaoh's own Ba, his eternal spirit. Located behind a set of sealed doors lay the remains that Cambyses had traveled so far to see. Ordering the mummified remains of Ahmose to be brought before him, Cambyses defiled the Pharaoh's corpse, demonstrating to the Egyptians that there was no place to hide, even in death, from the unmerciful revenge of the King of Kings, Cambyses.

However, the mummified corpse appeared impervious to the spears and lunges inflicted upon it by the Persian soldiers. Cambyses, filled with the rage of revenge and the heated despair at the defiant, seemingly immortal Pharaoh, finally had the remains burned on the dusty floor of the temple courtyard, a blasphemous action that was unheard of within Egyptian culture. This sacrilege served as one of the many mistakes made at the hand of Cambyses against the Egyptian people—and, unwittingly, his own people, the Persians. For it was said that fire itself was thought to be divine by the Persians, and therefore no human corpse should or could ever be presented to a god to be burned. As for the Egyptians, fire was an all-consuming living entity, one that would continue to consume all that it devoured until nothing was left. Neither the Persians nor the Egyptians permitted cremation of any corpses. With the charred remains of the deified Pharaoh's corpse slowly burning within the center of the inner courtyard, Cambyses had not only destroyed the eternal vessel for Ahmose's Ba, but had also irreversibly damaged his own reputation beyond repair, in front of his own people and those of his enemy, the Egyptians. However, even from the death of eternal destruction, Pharaoh Ahmose had one last trick to play on Cambyses, and had the truth ever been revealed to the Persian king at the time, who knows what untold harm and indignation he would have inflicted upon the Egyptians and his own armies. Ahmose, having learned from an Egyptian oracle that this undignified episode was to be administered upon his mummified corpse, had employed his son to place his true remains deeper in the recesses of the tomb, where they lay safe from the ravages of Cambyses's anger. Ahmose indeed had the last laugh.

One must bear in mind that at the time Herodotus first felt the warm sands of Egypt beneath his feet, nearly 75 years had passed since Cambyses had taken Egypt. The King of Kings, Cambyses had long been replaced as the occupying ruler when Herodotus walked and conversed with the high priests of Memphis. Artaxerxes I, the fifth King of Kings of Persia, was upon the throne, and ruled the Persian empire as far as the Black Sea in the north, to the arid deserts of Nubia in the south, to Libya in the west.

With this in mind, the historical chronicle continues in the ancient narrative of Herodotus, detailing the psychological effects upon the young Pharaoh Psammetichus, who, after his eventual safe release into exile, answered the call of monarchical ego and raised an army in a vain attempt to drive Cambyses out of Egypt. The move was completely futile, and proved to bring about the disastrous ending for the young Pharaoh, who ended his life by drinking a poison potion of bull's blood.

As for Cambyses, his embattled reign over the Egyptians was only just beginning. He left Zau having satisfied his revenge against Ahmose, but his lust for further dominion and expansion of his empire took hold of his senses. Having sent messages via courier to the four cardinal points, his vast armies were now becoming restless, and, given their size, they were depleting the meager resources of the Egyptian landscape to sustain the legions of men that were the cornerstone of Cambyses's quest for power. He set about conquering not only the Ethiopians to the south, but the belligerent Ammonians in the northwest as well as the Carthaginians in the far northwest, all of whom had snubbed his gracious offer of joining his kingdom as vassals to his court. The Phoenicians declined to participate in Cambyses's plans to attack Carthage by sea, on the basis that they had no intent of fighting their own sons. Cambyses had no other option but to withdraw his plans to bring the Carthaginians under Persian rule, as the volunteering Phoenicians were for all intents and purposes the backbone of his naval fleet. His opportunities dwindled rapidly.

Complete with his generals, captains, and hardened foot soldiers, Cambyses set off for the ancient Egyptian capital of Thebes in the south of Egypt (modern-day Luxor), some nine days' travel up river (the Nile flows south to north) from the northern capital of Memphis. The very home of Ra, the seat of kings, the Sheba of scriptures, vast wealth, and spoils awaited him and his men—or so he thought. Herodotus, together with other Greek historians, wrote of ancient Thebes:

> Not all proud Thebes unrivall'd walls contain,
>
> The world's great empress on th' Egyptian plain,
>
> That spreads her conquest o'er a thousand states,
>
> And pours her hero's through a hundred gates;
>
> Two hundred horsemen, and two hundred cars,
>
> From each wide portal issuing to the wars.
>
> —Pope

It was at Thebes that Cambyses split his army, based on the report by the "fish eaters"—a Greek ethnonym used to describe the sea coast inhabitants of the Gulf of Oman—after their return from clandestine activities in Ethiopia. Upon hearing of the refusal of gifts and peace under the auspices of Persian rule, Cambyses decided that he would lead his armies into Ethiopia himself and take it for his own. Misguided by blind greed, and an insatiable, abiding anger, he split his armies: The Greek mercenaries would stay behind in Egypt to control and keep the Egyptians from uprising, while 50,000 men on foot were sent to destroy the oracle of Zeus and enslave the Ammonians in what is today the Siwan oasis, just over 868 miles to the northwest of modern-day Luxor.

At the reports of the fish eaters brought to him from Ethiopia, Cambyses, ever true to his the ego-driven, manic lust for power, once again stoked the fires of rage within himself, and launched himself headlong into a string of military and strategic miscalculations. First, the King of Kings neglected to organize his troops and provisions correctly before embarking on his Ethiopian expedition, or so Herodotus regales us from within his Histories. If the figures are close to being correct, with regard to the size of the Ammonians campaign, and with the Greek contingent having been ordered to remain in Egypt, Cambyses would have taken much more than 50,000 men with him to Ethiopia. However, the exact figures are lacking in the history books, but the tales of hardship, tragedy, and mismanagement are plentiful. Having departed Thebes, Cambyses and his men would have taken the established trade routes presumably on the west bank of the Nile, frequenting the various watering holes en route. However, we are told that only a fifth of the way into his journey, he had already run out of supplies, and the men were forced to eat grass or whatever other vegetation they could collect.

Questions arise here as to what precautions the generals and captains had taken with regard to their men. The Ammonians' contingent would have traveled southward with the Ethiopian expedition until they parted ways at the opening in the Theban mountains, allowing them to head westward toward the Kharga oasis. From there the Ethiopian expedition would have continued toward the towns of Armant, then Esna and onward toward Silsila and Aswan—all contingent, of course, on whether they did indeed take the western bank as their route If, however, they had traveled on the eastern shores of the Nile, then they would have approached via the towns of Edfu, and then Silsila, Kom Ombo, and, finally, Aswan, recouping their loses and replenishing their depleted stores from Elephantine before heading southward into Nubia and the vast deserts between them and Ethiopia.

But again, only one fifth of the way in, we are told, tragedy hit them. After they ran out of supplies and provisions, they began to draw lots between themselves, killing and eating every 10th man to feed their hunger. Cambyses, fearful at the notion of cannibalism and with word returning to his Greek contingent in Egypt, he returned to Thebes having lost a major portion of his army, not to mention the respect of his men and his own ego.

As for the Ammonians campaign, herein lies the mystery. All accounts of this westward plodding army are shrouded in a cloak of ambiguity and intrigue. The 50,000-strong force arrived at the first oasis, the "Blessed Lakes," or so we are told. The forced march into the western desert had taken them seven long, hard, nearly unendurable days across the desert landscape from Thebes. From there, they would have crossed the great plateau and headed in a northerly direction toward the next oasis of modern-day Dakhla. From there, they would have continued to the next oasis of Farafra. And after a few days of rest and replenishment of their provisions, they would have continued to the last oasis, Bahariya, where they would then head west across the great desert itself, taking the small oasis of Jupiter by surprise and laying waste to its temples and Gods. However, the Ammonians state that the 50,000-strong armed forces of Cambyses arrived safely at the oasis of the Blessed Lakes, but after leaving, encountered a strong and powerful southerly wind that engulfed the entire army in a sandstorm.

The 50,000 were never to be seen or heard from again, vanishing completely off the face of history for all eternity.

One can easily imagine the never-ending train of men and livestock as they walked across the arid wastelands, file after file of men, shirtless, with little to shade them from the blistering heat of the Egyptian sun baking them in the western desert. Beads of sweat trickled down their raw, blistered backs, their shoulders slumped from the raw, bloody, open sores as the salty sweat entered their open, sun-scorched wounds. These broken men, their arms outstretched behind them, dragging their shields and spears, the very weight of them pulling them ever closer to the their stony graves. Fallen comrades lined the route as the train continued. As they continued the westward march, the rapping and tapping of spear ends and blades dragging across the stony desert floor is punctuated only by the intermittent sound of a metal tip hitting the soft, rotting flesh of a fallen solider. Bodies of dying men were unmoved by the alien touch of a spear gliding across the skin. Hands using the very last ounces of energy, reaching outward in vain attempts at catching the spear in the weak grip of the hand. Fingers aching and without feeling can do no more than merely touch the sharp tip as it is dragged across lifeless fingers. The spear tip, again dropping to the desert floor, continues with its usual rapping upon the stony surface unabated, as it is dragged further and further to the west and onward into the endless sands.

While such a scene is not hard to imagine, it is rather difficult to justify a force of 50,000 thousand men, along with their equipment, provisions, livestock, horses, and chariots, all disappearing overnight without a single trace left behind. Yet that is what we are led to believe happened, and it is this very myth that has driven many a European adventurer in search of the fabled army of Cambyses in the western deserts of Egypt. Some say they took a more southerly route around the Gilf el Kirbir, yet that would be nonsensical, militarily speaking, as the distance between the first oasis of Kharga, and the Gilf is quite considerable and in the completely wrong direction.

The devastating effects of the shifting dunes in the western desert become all too clear when viewing the vast towns that have re-emerged from antiquity after being buried for centuries beneath the sands. They have become small time capsules hidden in the sandy depths of time. Along the treacherous Darb el Arbein, loosely translated as the "40-day route" due to its lack of water for 40 days, the skeletal remains of not only humans, but camels, donkeys, dogs, cows, and other such like commodities simply lay in the open sun, bleached pure white over thousands of years of traffic along this well-trodden, harsh, and non-forgiving trade route. Thousands upon thousands of slaves died a meaningless death on these caravans of the damned, and their remains can still be seen to this very day. Yet, the question needs to be asked: Can 50,000 men afoot simply disappear without a trace?

There have been many reports that possible remains of the great armies of Cambyses have been located in the deserts of the western Saharan over the years. But, alas, they have proved to be erroneous. As of this writing no one has yet found the elusive 50,000-man army of Cambyses.

As for the Greek contingent, Cambyses, upon returning to Egypt, sent orders for them to return home. Having lost the Ammonians campaign as well as large swathes of his own Ethiopian battalion, he set sail northward down the Nile, returning to Memphis, where he could rule Egypt from the safety of its northern capital, surrounded by those who remained loyal to him as well as the remains of the once-great invading Persian army. However, as with most powerful ruling families of the time, sibling rivalry emerged upon the horizon of Cambyses's fragile kingdom, and he was forced to return to Persia. While en route, he fell victim to the very dagger that rattled beside him as he drove his chariot across the battlefield of Pelusium, where he destroyed the Maat of Egypt, and reduced her sovereign living God to a mere mortal man with nothing but sorrow and despair in his heart. While climbing upon his saddle, Cambyses's dagger penetrated deep into his thigh, severing his femoral artery and bringing a bloody end to the tyrannical rule and insatiable thirst for power of the King of Kings of Persia.

REFERENCES

Herodotus. *The Histories*. Revised edition by Aubrey De Sélincourt. London: Penguin Classics, 1996.

Olmstead, A.T. *History of the Persian Empire*. Chicago, Ill.: University of Chicago Press, 1948.

Shaw, Ian. *The Oxford History of Ancient Egypt*. New York: Oxford University Press, 2002.

Unholy Alliance: Ancient Astronauts and the New World Financial Order

By Jim Marrs

Throughout history the two most prominent methods for controlling the human population have been religion and finance. Could these well-honed, time-tested control mechanisms be of extraterrestrial origin?

Early humans, seeing the beauty and symmetry in nature, instinctively knew that some guiding force lay behind the order of life and so they developed a reverence for spiritual matters. Over time, however, and with advances in scientific knowledge, the material trappings and theologies of the various religions should have fallen away. But they haven't. Today, most of the world's population continues to follow one religion or another, often leading to conflicts, wars, and genocide. Moreover, most large, organized religions are intertwined with the acquisition of money. When did finance become so enmeshed in religion? What is it that has made religion so important in the minds of so many for so long?

One possibility is that religion may be based on a reality that has been lost today. According to the Old Testament, Sumerian tablets, and the accounts of the Greek and later Romans, there was a time when humans experienced face-to-face encounters with their gods. Virtually every ancient culture on this world told of legends of gods who came from the sky and taught them the fundamentals of civilization—language, mathematics, astronomy, chemistry, law, architecture, and finance.

Today, a growing number of researchers is taking the concept of ancient astronauts, the idea that non-humans visited the Earth millennia ago, more seriously. This concept was popularized in the 1970s by Swiss author Erich von Däniken and continues to find purchase in the popular imagination via the popular TV series. The evidence for such visitation—in sacred sites, ancient art, and anomalous artifacts—is quite compelling, in fact almost overwhelming, as detailed in the 2013 book *Our Occulted History*.

Our primitive ancestors felt awe and reverence for the technologically advanced visitors who came from the heavens. After all, no human could fly or perform feats that must have seemed like magic. The first humans thought of these visitors merely as Watchers or Messengers (angels) from the heavens. These visitors are referred to in the ancient tablets of Sumer as the *Anunnaki*, or "those who came to Earth from the heavens."

Rather than deal directly with the burgeoning human population, the ancient alien-gods ordained an administrative body or priesthood to pass along edicts and instruction as well as interpret policy. Once such clerics got a taste of wealth and power, they were loath to relinquish them. Religion soon evolved into a rigid structure of dogmas, catechisms, tithing, and obedience. Only after the Anunnaki appointed rulers over humanity did the concept of religion come into play.

According to researchers Peter Jiang and Jenny Li,

apparently, these extraterrestrials performed "great feats" in order to be worshipped as "gods." The reported next step was to provide technology to these Earth humans so that these humans could create impressive looking "rich" structures of religious worship, laid with gold and other mined mineral resources, of religious worship to these extraterrestrial "gods."[1]

By the time of the earliest recorded human civilizations, such as Sumer, Assyria, and Babylon, religions were well-established and had merged with the prevailing political structures of the time. These early civilizations firmly established the idea that the clergy could be the only religious authority and that kingship was a divine right. Anointed priests who worshipped one god exhorted their followers to demonize the worshipers of the others. And anyone who failed to offer allegiance to the one true god was castigated as a blasphemer, heathen, devil worshipper, or worse.

But something happened. Either through natural cataclysms or some prehistoric war, the planet, or at least the Near East, was devastated, and the ET gods withdrew from overt human contact. As the gods—the alien visitors—dropped from sight, the religions they created turned metaphysical. The concept of God evolved from a physical being to an omnipresent yet anthropomorphic supernatural entity. The elder conflicts between the ancient astronauts commandeering armies of human subjects were faithfully recorded in the Old Testament. These ancient wars became the metaphorical basis for the struggle between the new monotheistic God and his evil counterpart, Satan.

Baptist minister and author Paul Von Ward wrote about the development of supernatural religion beginning less than 3,000 years ago in Mesopotamia (now Iraq), the cradle of civilization: "Here religions that grew out of absentee-cults that described their gods as immortal, magical beings took the next step toward supernaturalism."[2]

Originally the term *Satan* merely meant any adversary of the gods. Princeton professor of religion Elaine Pagels argues that Satan came to represent human hostility against other humans: "And it's no accident that the foundational texts of Christian tradition—the gospels of the New Testament, like the Dead Sea Scrolls—all begin with stories of Satan contending against God's spirit." Pagels goes on to explain that Christians later "turned the image of Satan against a far wider range of targets—against the Roman empire and its government, which persecuted Christians, and then against other 'intimate enemies'—other Christians, whom they called 'heretics.'"[3] Von Ward elaborates on Pagels' idea by writing, "[H]istory makes it clear that the Hebrews had simply followed the example of their patron god. They labeled their opponents, foreign or domestic, Satanic worshipers of Beelzebub, Belial, and the Princes of Darkness. In return, their opponents likely shouted their own epithets of 'infidel' (meaning 'unfaithful to the "true" god')."[4]

Various historical events provided the basis for Western supernaturalism near the end of the Roman Empire. These events included the development of absentee non-human cult worship in the Middle East; the Hebrew worship of *Yahweh*, who was believed to be the leader of the gods of old; and the new and compelling reformation cult of Jesus of Nazareth. Von Ward attributes the rise of supernaturalism to the simultaneous rise of powerful institutions—for instance, the development of Roman organizational skills and the creation of a Christ-centered church, the power of Rome to elevate St. Paul's Christian cult to the status of the state religion, and the Nicean council of bishops that "culled from competing texts a Bible that largely excludes references to the reality of other [Advanced Beings] and Jesus' humanity."[5]

Generations of humans slowly developed a defense mechanism once the ancient gods were no longer visible:

> The Anunnaki had apparently decided to go about their own affairs, but humans felt bereft at being deserted. So supernatural theology was the defense mechanism created to help cope with the pain and anxiety of an obvious separation of humans from their gods. One of its purposes was to assure humans that the religious rituals would either bring the departed gods back to Earth or reconnect the humans to them in the supernatural realm."[6]

Furthermore, in both early Eastern and Western cultures, rulers gained power and wealth from religion. But, beginning with the Enlightenment and the advent of the printing press, religion waned, especially in highly developed nations. Today, the favored control mechanism is through the lending of money. Author Joseph P. Farrell saw the rapid development of the private issuance of bullion-based monies both in ancient times and in various cultures as suggesting "the evident hand of a hidden international class of bullion-brokers, war merchants, slave traders, and mining operators, for almost invariably, the pattern is the same."[7] This pattern involved blending finance with the prevailing religion, as if money itself were God-ordained. It remains a powerful control mechanism over humanity today.

Farrell has argued that the methodology of aligning religion with money went something like this: Rulers would penetrate and ally with the temple, issue false receipts, substitute bullion for letters of credit as a measure against the false receipts, and thus create a facsimile of money.

Thus, we arrive back at the state of issuing false receipts, only in this instance, these receipts are neither false nor counterfeit, they are simply privately created notes or promises to pay a certain amount of bullion (which they also control). Thus, once again the money supply is not only expanded, but the use of such instruments actually served to allow the bullion brokers to circulate more of such notes than they had actual bullion to redeem. The key, once again, was the sanctifying probity that the temple association gave them. With this step their power and influence over the various states which they penetrated was almost complete, for it gave these ancient bankers, like their modern counterparts, the ability to expand or contract a state's money supply and to control their economies to create boom or bust.[8]

The power of exchanging money can be traced back to the Near East, where people called money changers were prevalent, exchanging the currencies of the various cities and nations into money acceptable to the temple priests. Money therefore became closely connected to the temples of religion, which also doubled as centers for the study of astronomy and astrology. Recall that it was only in the temple at Jerusalem that Jesus, the "Prince of Peace," turned violent—and this was against the money changers. The conflict between the money changers and the human population has continued through the ages.

Despite popular myth, the American colonial revolt against England occurred more over concern for its own currency than a small tax on tea. During a visit to Britain in 1763, Benjamin Franklin explained the prosperity of the American colonists by stating,

> That is simple. In the colonies, we issue our own money. It is called Colonial Scrip. We issue it in proper proportion to the demands of trade and industry to make the products pass easily from the producers to the consumers. In this manner, creating for ourselves our own paper money, we control its purchasing power, and we have no interest to pay to no one.[9]

However, under pressure from the bankers, King George III of England ordered that all colonies must abandon Colonial Scrip and deal only in interest-bearing British pound. Franklin later explained,

> The colonies would gladly have borne the little tax on tea and other matters had it not been that England took away from the colonies their money, which created unemployment and dissatisfaction. The inability of colonists to get power to issue their own money permanently out of the hands of George III and the international bankers was the prime reason for the Revolutionary War.[10]

By the mid-1800s, the bankers of Europe—predominately the banking dynasty of Mayer Amschel Rothschild—had spread worldwide, despite their setback in North America due to the American Revolution. But they didn't give up in their attempts to regain control of the United States; in fact, they may have been instrumental in influencing the course of events leading to civil war.

For some years, the Rothschilds had financed major projects in the United States on both sides of the Mason-Dixon Line. Nathan Rothschild, who owned a large Manchester textile plant, bought his cotton from Southern interests and financed the importation of Southern cotton prior to the war. At the same time, wrote Rothschild biographer Derek Wilson, "He had made loans to various states of the Union, and had been, for a time, the official European banker for the U.S. government and was a pledged supporter of the Bank of the United States."[11]

The War Between the States was fought more over economics than slavery, despite how modern political correctness aims to convince otherwise. And it was encouraged through secret societies, especially the Knights of the Golden Circle, one member of which was the assassin of President Abraham Lincoln. The Knights organization was founded in 1854 by Dr. George W.L. Bickley and was patterned on the Freemasons. Bickley reportedly was an agent for Nathan Rothschild, who controlled the Bank of England. Lincoln himself made it clear that his "paramount object in this struggle is to save the Union, and is not either to save or to destroy slavery. If I could save the Union without freeing any slave, I would do it; and if I could save it by freeing all the slaves, I would do it; and if I could save it by freeing some and leaving others alone, I would also do that."[12]

German Chancellor Otto von Bismarck once explained,

The division of the United States into federations of equal force was decided long before the Civil War by the high

financial powers of Europe. These bankers were afraid that
the United States, if they remained in one block and as one
nation, would attain economic and financial independence,
which would upset their financial domination over the world.
The voice of the Rothschilds prevailed.... Therefore they sent
their emissaries into the field to exploit the question of slavery and to open an abyss between the two sections of the
Union.[13]

In need of money to fund the war effort, Lincoln did not borrow from the European banks as expected. In 1862, he issued about
$450 million in currency printed with green ink called "Greenbacks."
This paper money, legalized by an act of Congress with nothing to
back it, was debt-free, *fiat money* (currency declared legal). Lincoln
saw the debt-free creation of money as government's greatest cre-
ative opportunity. But he may have forgotten that the first assassination attempt on an American president was in 1835 against Andrew Jackson, who incurred the wrath of the international bankers
by abolishing the country's central bank. Lincoln also found it was
fatal to cross the international bankers. He was shot by John Wilkes
Booth while attending Ford's Theatre on April 14, 1865, and died the
next morning. (It should be noted here that President John F. Kennedy also issued interest-free money by authorizing $4.3 billion in
silver-backed "United States Notes" in mid-1963. Kennedy, too, was
shot in the head in public.)

The money changers of Europe gained even greater power during World War I when many of Europe's royal houses lost their
leadership positions. Their greatest fear came with the rise of communism in Russia. Although the Bolsheviks were aided in their revolution against the Czar by western bankers, their control slipped
when Stalin ascended to dictatorial power following Lenin's death in
1924. With the success of the Bolshevik Revolution, wealthy and titled Russians fled to western nations warning of the dangers to capitalism from international communism. Great fear was engendered

among the wealthy. The cry of "Workers of the world unite!" reverberated within communists parties from Berlin and Paris to London and New York.

It may well have been the post–World War I plan of the banker elite to create a socialist East and pit it against the capitalist West, but the fear of the spread of communism caused a change in plans. Something had to be done to halt the spread of communist socialism and Germany was in a central position to act as a barrier. However, something first had to be done with the democratic Weimar Republic in Germany. One solution was to combine American capitalism with German corporations in the 1920s under the Dawes Plan and the Young Plan, which were plans to help Germany repay its debt after World War I. These plans used American loans to create and consolidate the German steel and chemical giants, Vereinigte Stahlwerke and I.G. Farben, both major supporters of the fledgling Nazi Party.

The final solution was to finance an Austrian Army corporal who was drawing pay as an undercover agent for his military superiors after failed attempts as an artist. This, of course, was Adolf Hitler, who gained power through the backing of both the occult Thule Society, composed of German aristocrats and wealthy industrialists, as well as Western banking interests. One of the largest lenders of money to the Nazis was National City Bank of New York (now Citicorp), then headed by John J. McCloy, who became the U.S. High Commissioner of Germany after the war. Over the course of several years, the former corporal brought his National Socialist German Workers Party (the Nazis) from a handful of members to a national organization of millions.

In early 1933, Hitler was elected chancellor of Germany. In 1934, with the death of President Paul von Hindenburg, Hitler consolidated his office with that of president and assumed the title of *fuehrer*, or leader over the entire nation. But then Hitler made a fatal error—the same one that may have cost the lives of Lincoln and Kennedy. He failed to follow the wishes of the moneyed elite to borrow money from the international bankers. Instead, he issued his own debt-free money, *Reichmarks*, and put the Germans back to work on public projects such as the autobahn highway system and the production of war materials.

In early Nazi meetings, Hitler had listened to the views of German economist Gottfied Feder, who advocated monetary control through a nationalized central bank rather than private banks and that financial interests had enslaved the population by controlling the money supply. One of the platforms of the Nazi Party was the breaking of debt-slavery—in other words, interest payments. Writing in his book *Mein Kampf,* Hitler stated,

> Germany's development already stood before my eyes too clearly for me not to know that the hardest battle had to be fought, not against hostile nations, but rather against international capital.... The fight against international finance and loan capital has become the most important point in the program of the German nation's fight for its independence and freedom.[14]

In 1933, Germany, like America, was in the depths of the Great Depression. A large segment of the population was out of work, and the money hyper-inflated. Many recall the stories of Germans needing a wheelbarrow loaded with paper money to buy a single loaf of bread. By the time of the 1936 Berlin Olympics—a mere three years later—Germany had become an economic powerhouse, with near-full employment and stable money thanks to its freedom from the international bankers. However, the wealthy elite, who traced their money management secrets back to ancient Sumer, could not afford to have the rest of the world see the benefits of interest-free money, as sought by Benjamin Franklin, Thomas Jefferson, and many others throughout history. Winston Churchill, a member of the aristocratic and wealthy elite, summed up their reaction to Hitler's actions prior to World War II when he stated, "You must understand that this war is not against Hitler or National Socialism but against the [economic] strength of the German people, which must be smashed once and for all, regardless whether it is in the hands of Hitler or a Jesuit priest."[15]

The Germans lost the war, but the wealthy elite, who had funded Hitler and created the Nazis, did not. In fact, in many ways, they won. The Nazis experimented with new technology in nuclear science, weaponry, energy manipulation, psychiatric drugs, and innovative techniques of propaganda and mind control, all of which helped the elite. They learned the best way to overthrow nations, how to dumb down populations with propaganda enhanced by fluoride and other chemical agents, and how to insinuate fear, torture, and assassination into a civilized society.

They brought these tactics, along with thousands of unrepentant Nazis, to America under a variety of programs, including Operation Paperclip, which recruited former Nazi scientists and brought them to the United States. All of this helped them create their new National Security police state. This infiltration of unreconstructed Nazis was largely overseen by banker John J. McCloy and his protégé, Allen Dulles, who as CIA director whitewashed the Nazis records. Both McCloy and Dulles sat on the Warren Commission, hand-picked by President Lyndon B. Johnson to investigate the assassination of President Kennedy.

One of the hidden tools of elitist financial control may be the Exchange Stabilization Fund (ESF) of the United States Treasury. This little-known agency is one of those government constructs that has morphed into a gigantic money-moving operation with absolutely no oversight by the federal government, the states, or the American people. Yet the ESF uses tax money and its profits to fund operations both inside and outside the country. Texas Congressman Henry B. Gonzalez, a vocal opponent of the Fed, while chairman of the House Banking Committee criticized the ESF for "back-door financing," and "a complete lack of public accountability."[16]

The ESF was created and originally financed by the Gold Reserve Act of 1934. Its purpose, according to an official description, was "to contribute to exchange rate stability and counter disorderly conditions in the foreign exchange market." The act authorized the secretary of the treasury to exclusively deal in gold, foreign exchange, securities, and instruments of credit subject to the approval of the president. This all sounds fine until one learns that it allows the U.S. treasury secretary to operate outside U.S. laws. According to minority members of the House Committee on Coinage, Weights, and Measures who reviewed this law in its preparation,

> This [law] in fact, means that the Secretary of the Treasury shall be under no obligation to comply with general laws of the United States in the handling of this fund.... We believe that [this] places autocratic and dictatorial power in the hands of one man directly over the control of the value of money and credit and indirectly over prices.... We believe that this is too great a power to place in the hands of any one man. We believe that it is contrary to every true principle of American Government.[17]

When ownership of gold was outlawed for Americans in 1933, the ESF transferred gold out of the country to foreigners in exchange for dollars, in turn draining our gold reserves for years to come. Today when people blame the Federal Reserve for stealing America's gold reserves, they should know that it was actually the ESF, that agency never scrutinized or questioned by Congress, that drained the Federal Reserve many years ago.

After the war, the ESF helped design the world's new monetary system, including its best-known creations: the International Monetary Fund (IMF) and the World Bank. The ESF also has been charged with providing unaccountable funds to the CIA. According to Lawrence Houston, the first general counsel of the CIA, "The heart and soul of covert operations is...the provisions of un-vouchered funds, and the inviolability of such funds from outside inspection."[18]

Now the ESF has copycat agencies in many states and itself has become nothing more than a slush fund with connections to CIA black operations. There are even accusations of laundering drug money. The slush funds operate outside of legislative oversight and public scrutiny and, though technically legal, outside of the intentions of the U.S. Constitution and Bill of Rights. To pinpoint the movement of tax money to questionable recipients would require a full audit of all the Economic Stabilization Funds and the legislation that regulates transfers of public tax monies to innumerable, clandestine, and questionable, though technically legalized, funds.

Internet commentator Eric deCarbonnel documented an immense amount of information on the ESF and concluded the agency

> controls the New York Fed, runs the CIA's black budget, and is the architect of the world's monetary system (IMF, World Bank, etc). ESF financing (through the OSS and then the CIA) built up the worldwide propaganda network which has so badly distorted history today (including erasing awareness of its existence from popular consciousness). It has been directly involved in virtually every major U.S. fraud/scandal since its creation in 1934: the London gold pool, the Kennedy assassinations, Iran-Contra, CIA drug trafficking, HIV, and worse....[19]

Another little-known mechanism for financial control is the Financial Stability Board (FSB), an outgrowth of the Financial Stability Forum, once a part of the Nazi-dominated Bank for International Settlements. President Obama signed the United States on as a member of the FSB during the G-20 meeting of the nations' finance ministers in April 2009. Critics claim this board of foreign central bankers, in the name of financial stability, now can dictate financial policy to such U.S. institutions as the Federal Reserve System, the Securities & Exchange Commission, and others.

Though the FSB only began in 2009, and the ESF, during the Great Depression, as previously noted the history of banking control goes much further back. Dr. Mujahid Kamran, vice chancellor of the University of Punjab and an expert on corporate America, has concluded that the American banking system is ultimately pernicious. As he writes in *The Grand Deception—Corporate America and Perpetual War*:

> The advent of the industrial revolution, the invention of a banking system based on usury, and scientific and technological advancements during the past three centuries have had three major consequences. These have made the incredible concentration of wealth in a few hands possible, have led to the construction of increasingly deadly weapons culminating in weapons of mass destruction, and have made it possible to mold the minds of vast populations by application of scientific techniques through the media and control of the educational system. The wealthiest families on planet earth call the shots in every major upheaval that they cause. Their sphere of activity extends over the entire globe, and even beyond, their ambition and greed for wealth and power knows no bounds, and for them, most of mankind is garbage—"human garbage." It is also their target to depopulate the globe and maintain a much lower population compared to what we have now.[20]

Dr. Kamran also noted that universities in developing countries operate in close partnership with the large private foundations, and that the only way to truly understand the operation of the world is "to realize the U.S. Government is owned by those who own these foundations."[21]

If the idea that a small group of international yet interconnected individuals control the worlds of finance and commerce seems like a paranoid conspiracy theory, consider a 2011 study by three scientists at the Swiss Federal Institute of Technology in Zurich. Combining mathematics used to model natural systems with comprehensive corporate data, they traced the ownership of the transnational corporations. From a database of 37 million companies and investors, the Swiss team constructed a model of which companies controlled others through shareholding networks, coupled with each company's operating revenues, to map the structure of economic power. Shockingly, the study confirmed the worst fears of conspiracy theorists and the Occupy Wall Street protestors, as their analysis of the relationships among 43,000 transnational corporations identified a relatively small group of companies—primarily banks—with disproportionate power over the global economy.

According to an article in *New Scientist*, the study

revealed a core of 1,318 companies with interlocking ownerships. Each of the 1,318 had ties to two or more other companies, and on average they were connected to 20. What's more, although they represented 20 per cent of global operating revenues, the 1,318 appeared to collectively own through their shares the majority of the world's large blue chip and manufacturing firms—the 'real' economy—representing a further 60 per cent of global revenues.[22]

The study further untangled the web of ownership, discovering much of it tracked back to a "super-entity" of 147 even more tightly knit companies—all of their ownership was held by other members of the super-entity—that controlled 40 percent of the total wealth in the network. Most of these firms were financial institutions. The top 20 included Barclays Bank, JPMorgan Chase & Co, and The Goldman Sachs Group. As Dr. James B. Glattfelder of the Swiss Federal Institute of Technology, and one of the authors of the study, explained, "In effect, less than one per cent of the companies were able to control 40 per cent of the entire network."[23] Although study members and commentators disparaged talk of conspiratorial control, they did admit that such centralized interconnectedness was worrisome as it could cause instability in world markets.

THE BLOOD THAT RULES

But the Swiss researchers limited their study only to official corporate data. They did not seek to determine the family, social, and business relationships between owners and stockholders. Yet, personal relationships *do* matter, especially in matters of business and politics. Beginning with the Sumerians, Egyptians, and Romans, the leadership of royal families and major corporations has been determined by how closely one was connected to certain bloodlines. Though times have changed drastically since the time of the Habsburgs, the Romanovs, and the Rothschilds, it appears the person closest to the ancient bloodlines seems to always carry the day, especially in United States national elections. In every election the candidate with the most royal genes always wins.

Mainstream news reports in 2000 quoted researchers at *Burke's Peerage* as predicting George W. Bush would win the presidency over Al Gore because, although both Bush and Gore were related and of royal blood, the Bush family was the more closely connected. "[Bush] is closely related to every European Monarch both on and off the throne," said Burke's publishing director, Harold Brooks-Baker. "Not one member of [Bush's] family was working class, middle class, or even middle, middle class," he added.[24]

British conspiracy author David Icke, citing information from *Burke's Peerage,* wrote,

Every presidential election in America, since and including George Washington in 1789 to Bill Clinton, has been won by the candidate with the most British and French royal genes. Of the 42 presidents to Clinton, 33 have been related to two people: Alfred the Great, King of England, and Charlemagne, the most famous monarch of France. So it goes on: 19 of them are related to England's Edward III, who has 2,000 blood connections to Prince Charles. The same goes with the banking families in America. George Bush and Barbara Bush are from the same bloodline—the Pierce bloodline, which changed its name from Percy, when it crossed the Atlantic. Percy is one of the aristocratic families of Britain, to this day.[25]

In case anyone should think that Barack Hussein Obama must be an exception to these bloodline connections, they would be wrong. According to Lynne Cheney, wife of Dick Cheney, Obama is an eighth cousin to the former vice president. She discovered this familial connection while researching her ancestry for a book. According to a Cheney spokesperson, Obama is a descendent of Mareen Duvall, a French Huguenot whose son married the granddaughter of a Richard Cheney, who had arrived in Maryland in the late 1650s from England.[26]

Moreover, the *New York Post* reported that both Obama and Cheney are blood relations to the Bush family. According to the paper, George W. Bush and Obama are 10th cousins once removed. They are linked through a 17th-century Massachusetts couple, Samuel Hinckley and Sarah Soole. Hinckley is a distant relative of George Herbert Walker Bush's friend John Warnock Hinckley Sr., whose son, John Warnock Hinckley Jr., shot President Ronald Reagan in 1981.[27]

Gary Boyd Roberts, a former senior research scholar at the New England Historic Genealogical Society, has traced George W. Bush's family tree to 15 U.S. presidents including George Washington, Millard Fillmore, Franklin Pierce, Abraham Lincoln, Ulysses Grant, Rutherford B. Hayes, James Garfield, Grover Cleveland, Theodore Roosevelt, William H. Taft, Calvin Coolidge, Herbert Hoover, Franklin D. Roosevelt, Richard Nixon, and Gerald Ford.

Moreover, the Bush family, according to several sources, is closely related to the king of Albania, and has kinship with every member of the British royal family and the House of Windsor. They are related to 20 British dukes, the 13th cousin of Britain's Queen Mother, and of her daughter Queen Elizabeth. George W. is 13th cousin once removed from Prince Charles and has direct descent from King Henry III, Charles II, and Edward I of England. According to *Burke's Peerage*, even former President Bill Clinton is genetically related to the House of Windsor.

Many are unaware that the Windsors, the royal family of England, originally were known by their German name Sachsen-Coburg und Gotha, a German dynasty shortened to Saxe-Coburg-Gotha. The change to Windsor came during World War I when England was at war with Germany and there was considerable anti-German sentiment. To distance themselves from their German heritage, on July 17, 1917, Queen Victoria's grandson King George V officially declared that all male descendants of Queen Victoria would bear the name Windsor. The name Windsor came from a castle owned by the family. Six British monarchs, including Queen Victoria and King George III, who ruled during the American Revolution, were members of the German House of Hanover. In 1960, Queen Elizabeth II, along with her husband, Prince Philip, the son of Alice of Battenberg, announced his name would henceforth be Anglicized to Philip Mountbatten.

Phillip Eugene de Rothschild, a descendant of the Rothschilds now living in America, once explained that the German Battenberg bloodline is joined with the Bauer-Rothschild bloodline in a "Rothsburg dynasty" that traces their ancestry back to Aeneas. In Greek and Roman mythology, Aeneas was a Trojan soldier who was said to be a human hybrid, son of the goddess Venus as well as the father of Romulus and Remus, the founders of Rome.

It has been reported from several sources that the Rothschilds believe themselves descended from the Sumerian God-King Nimrod, reportedly the great-grandson of the biblical Noah. According to the prestigious genealogical publication *Burke's Peerage*, one Rothschild child born in 1922 was named Albert Anselm Salomon Nimrod Rothschild.

Several researchers have traced the ancient bloodlines of the ancient astronauts, the *Anunnaki*, as they spread from Sumer, Babylon, Egypt, and even China to encompass the entire world. Although conventional history has concentrated on the male descendants of these bloodlines, through the centuries the bloodline actually has been passed through the mitochondrial DNA of the females. The passing of the true bloodline has primarily been done through incest and intermarrying, as practiced by most of history's rulers, though an extended network of relations also has been created through concubines, mistresses, slaves, hired help, and even rape.

A growing number of researchers and writers are building the case against a mere handful of individuals apparently obsessed with maintaining the privileges of their bloodline. They appear more intent on creating a New World Order based on privilege and control rather than helping the world develop individual worth, creativity, and productivity. The strategy and practices of such a banking elite coupled with religion since ancient times has involved slavery—whether physical or financial—war, starvation, usurpation of the money-creating power of the state, the invention of debt-as-money, and economic cycles based on astrological alignments. But whether spiritual, metaphysical, or physical, such control mechanisms appear to have originated from beyond the material world.

NOTES

1. From *www.agoracosmopolitan.com/home/Frontpage/2007/01/26/ 01340.html*.
2. From Paul Von Ward, *We Have Never Been Alone*. Charlottesville, VA: Hampton Roads Publishing Company, 2011, p. 285.
3. From *www.tannerlectures.utah.edu/lectures/documents/Pagels99.pdf*.
4. From Von Ward, *Princes of Darkness*, p. 47.
5. Ibid.
6. From Von Ward, *We Have Never Been Alone*, p. 287.

7. From Joseph P. Farrell, *Babylon's Banksters: The Alchemy of Deep Physics, High Finance and Ancient Religion*. Port Townsend, Wash.: Feral House, 2010, p. 295.

8. Farrell, p. 204.

9. From *www.opednews.com/articles/How-Benjamin-Franklin-Caus-by-Mike-Kirchubel-110711-773.html*.

10. Ibid.

11. From Derek Wilson, *Rothschild: The Wealth and Power of a Dynasty*. New York: Charles Scribner's Sons, 1988, p. 178.

12. From Thomas R. Dye and L. Harmon Zeigler, *The Irony of Democracy: An Uncommon Introduction to American Politics*. Belmont, Calif.: Duxbury Press, 1975, p. 83.

13. From G. Edward Griffin, *The Creature From Jekyll Island*. Westlake Village, Calif.: American Media, 1994, p. 374.

14. Adolf Hitler, *Mein Kampf*. New York: Houghton Mifflin Company, 1940, pp. 287–288.

15. Emrys Hughes, *Winston Churchill: British Bulldog—His Career in War and Peace*. New York: Exposition Press, 1955, p. 145.

16. "Treasury sets up two-billion fund for stabilization." *The New York Times* (May 1, 1934), p. 1.

17. C. Randall Henning, *The Exchange Stabilization Fund: Slush Money or War Chest?* Washington, D.C.: Institute for International Economics, 1999, p. 12.

18. Eric de Carbonnel, "The Exchange Stabilization Fund Role in Financing CIA Covert Operations," *Market Skeptics*, Sept. 4, 2010: *www.marketskeptics.com/2010/09/exchange-stabilization-fund-role-in.html*.

19. Ibid.

20. From *www.newdawnmagazine.com/articles/who-really-controls-the-world*.

21. Ibid.

22. Andy Coghlan and Debora MaxKensie, "Revealed—The Capitalist Network That Runs the World," *New Scientist* (Oct. 24, 2011): *www.newscientist.com/article/mg21228354.500-revealed-the-capitalist-network-that-runs-the-world.html.*

23. Ibid.

24. Tony Eufinger, "Royal Red Carpet Is Path to White House," *ABC News,* Oct. 25, 2000: *http://abcnews.go.com/International/story?id=82279&page=1#.TzgcsFF7R8E.*

25. From *www.atlanteanconspiracy.com/2008/06/presidential-bloodlines.html.*

26. "Lynne Cheney: VP, Obama Are Eighth Cousins," *NBC News* (Oct. 17, 2007).

27. Hasani Gittens, "Dissing Cousins: Obama, Cheney, Bush Related," *New York Post* (Oct. 17, 2007): *www.nypost.com/P/News/Regional/Item_Kjxdkmwzqbghpdxxdgwnep.*

INDEX

About the Contributors

Thomas Brophy has a PhD in physics from the University of Colorado, was a research scientist at the Laboratory for Atmospheric and Space Physics, Boulder, with NASA interplanetary spacecraft projects, and was a National Science Foundation exchange scientist with the University of Tokyo and Japan Space Program. He then recombined his interests in fundamental physical theory with practice and philosophy of ancient contemplative traditions to include the non-calculable and immeasurable aspects of reality, teaching integral philosophy, managing and developing a unique forefront research and teaching institute in southern California, and writing his book *The Mechanism Demands a Mysticism*. The combination of integral philosophy with astrophysical dynamics led to his studies of the astroarchaeology of prehistoric and protohistoric Egypt, and to his books *The Origin Map*, *Black Genesis: The Prehistoric Origins of Ancient Egypt*, and *Imhotep the African* (coauthored with Robert Bauval). He also worked in the IT/telecommunications industry, and found application for mathematical methods in gaming and investment theory. He has published peer-reviewed scientific articles in premier journals including *Icarus*, *Mediterranean Journal of Archaeology and Archaeometry*, *IEEE Journal*, and *Science*. He has been a featured presenter at scientific conferences and integral spirituality symposia in the United States, Europe, and Asia. He now teaches integral theory and related topics, and is small business owner.

Dr. Ardy Sixkiller Clarke, professor emeritus at Montana State University, was a professor of educational leadership and the director of the Center for Bilingual/Multicultural Education for 30 years. During those years, she collected nearly 1,000 stories from indigenous people throughout the Americas, the South Pacific, New Zealand, and Australia about their ancient stories and interactions with star people and encounters with UFOs. She is the author of two nonfiction books, *Encounters with Star People: Untold Stories of American Indians* and *Sisters in the Blood: The Education of Women in Native America*, and 12 children's books. You may view Dr. Clarke's Website at *www.sixkiller.com* or contact her at ardy@sixkiller.com.

Micah Hanks is a writer, researcher, lecturer, and radio personality whose work addresses a variety of areas, including history, politics, scientific theories, and unexplained phenomena. Open-minded but skeptical in his approach, his research has examined a broad variety of subjects over the years, incorporating interest in cultural studies, natural science, and scientific anomalies, and the prospects of our technological future as a species as influenced by science. A weekly podcast that follows his research is available at his popular Website, *www.gralienreport.com*. Hanks lives in the heart of Appalachia near Asheville, North Carolina.

Frank Joseph has authored more books about the lost civilization of Atlantis than any other writer in history. His complete published output includes 26 titles in as many foreign editions. He was the editor in chief of *Ancient American*, a popular science magazine, from its inception in 1993 until his retirement 14 years later. During his career as a staff reporter for other periodicals, Joseph interviewed Secretary of State John Kerry, Minnesota governor Jesse Ventura, test pilot Chuck Jaeger, soprano Sumi Jo, symphonic conductor George Solti, and actors Peter Ustinov, Vincent Price, and Shirley McLaine. Today, he is a feature writer for *Atlantis Rising* as well as Australia's *Nexus* and *New Dawn*. A scuba diver since he was 17 years old, Joseph has participated in hundreds of underwater expeditions from the Eastern Mediterranean Sea and the Atlantic Ocean off North Africa to the Bahamas and Polynesia. A professor of world archaeology at Japan's Savant Society, his work has received award recognition from the Midwest Epigraphic Society, the Burrows Cave Society, and the Ancient American Artifact Preservation Society. He lives today with his wife, Laura, and Norwegian Forest Cat, Sammy, in the Upper Mississippi Valley.

Jim Marrs is a Texas journalist and author of four *New York Times* best-selling books. His latest book, *Our Occulted History,* concerns the origins of humankind and the possibility of extraterrestrial intervention.

A native of Fort Worth, Texas, Jim Marrs earned a degree in journalism from the University of North Texas and attended graduate school at Texas Tech in Lubbock. He has worked for several Texas newspapers, including the *Fort Worth Star-Telegram*, where beginning in 1968 he served as a police reporter and general assignments reporter covering stories locally, in Europe, and in the Middle East. After a leave of absence to serve with a Fourth Army Intelligence Unit during the Vietnam War, he became a military and aerospace writer and an investigative reporter.

Beginning in1976 until his retirement in 2007, Marrs taught a course on the assassination of President John F. Kennedy at the University of Texas at Arlington. In 1989, his book *Crossfire: The Plot That Killed Kennedy* was published to critical acclaim and reached the *New York Times* Paperback Non-Fiction Best-Seller List in February 1992. It became a basis for the Oliver Stone film *JFK*. Marrs served as a chief consultant for both the film's screenplay and production. An updated and expanded version was published in 2013.

In May 1997, Marrs's in-depth investigation of UFOs, *Alien Agenda*, was published and eventually translated into several foreign languages, becoming the top-selling nonfiction UFO book in the world. From 2000 to 2007, he taught a course on UFOs at the University of Texas at Arlington, becoming perhaps the first to teach about UFOs at the college level.

Marrs has won several Associated Press writing and photography awards, including the Aviation/Aerospace Writer's Association National Writing Award and Newsmaker of the Year Award from the Fort Worth chapter of the Society of Professional Journalists. In 1993, Marrs received *Freedom* magazine's Human Rights Leadership Award. His other books include *Rule by Secrecy* (2000), *The Terror Conspiracy Revisited* (2007), *The Rise of the Fourth Reich* (2008), and *The Trillion-Dollar Conspiracy* (2010).

Marrs has appeared on ABC, NBC, CBS, CNN, CSPAN, and the Discovery, Learning, and History Channels; *Good Morning America, Geraldo, Montel Williams, Today, Tech TV,* and *Larry King Live*; and on the *George Noory, Art Bell, Alex Jones,* and *Jeff Rensel* programs, among many others.

Nick Redfern works full time as an author, lecturer, and journalist. He writes about a wide range of unsolved mysteries, including Bigfoot, UFOs, the Loch Ness Monster, alien encounters, ancient civilizations, and government conspiracies. His books include *Close Encounters of the Fatal Kind; For Nobody's Eyes Only; Monster Files; The World's Weirdest Places; The Pyramids and the Pentagon; Keep Out!; The Real Men in Black; The NASA Conspiracies; Contactees;* and *Memoirs of a Monster Hunter.* He writes regularly for *Cryptomundo.com,* the *Mutual UFO Network Journal,* and *Mysterious Universe.* He has appeared on numerous television shows, including Fox News; History Channel's *Ancient Aliens, MonsterQuest,* and *UFO Hunters;* VH1's *Legend Hunters;* National Geographic Channel's *The Truth About UFOs* and *Paranatural;* BBC's

Out of this World; MSNBC's *Countdown*; and SyFy Channel's *Proof Positive*. Nick lives just a few miles from the infamous grassy knoll in Dallas, Texas. He can be contacted at his blog: *http://nickredfernfortean.blogspot.com.*

Scott Alan Roberts is the founder and publisher of *Intrepid Magazine* (*www.intrepidmag.com*), a journal dedicated to politics, science, culture, ufology, unexplained phenomena, alternative fringe theories, and world mysteries. He is the founder of the Paradigm Symposiums (*www.paradigmsymposium.com*), which was hailed by Philip Coppens as the "number-one alternative conference in the United States, if not the world."

As an accomplished illustrator and designer, Scotty has spent the bulk of the last three decades in advertising and publishing. He is a historian, theologian, researcher, student of Egyptology, and stalwart opponent of Big-S Skepticism, enjoying his role as a "stand-up philosopher." Scotty attended bible college and theological seminary, and worked as a youth pastor for several years alongside his career in advertising and independent comic book publishing. He co-created the highly successful Ancient Heroes trading card series, and began development on a line of young readers books. He authored and illustrated his first historical novel, *The Rollicking Adventures of Tam O'Hare* (*www.tamohare.com*), an anthropomorphized historical novel set in Tudor England, Ireland, and Scotland, which garnered broad attention with teen and college readers.

Scotty is the author of *The Rise and Fall of the Nephilim: The Untold Story of Fallen Angels, Giants on the Earth and Their Extraterrestrial Origins*, and *The Secret History of the Reptilians: The Pervasive Presence of the Serpent in Human History, Religion and Alien Mythos*. Scotty lives with his wife and children just across the Minnesota border in rural Wisconsin, where he remains an avid Vikings fan and a stranger in a strange land.

Robert M. Schoch, a full-time faculty member at the College of General Studies at Boston University since 1984, earned his PhD (1983) in geology and geophysics at Yale University.

In the early 1990s, Dr. Schoch stunned the world with his revolutionary research that recast the date of the Great Sphinx of Egypt to a period thousands of years earlier than its standard attribution. In demonstrating that the leonine monument has been heavily eroded by water—despite the fact that its location on the edge of the Sahara has endured hyper-arid climactic conditions for the past 5,000 years—Schoch revealed to the world that humanity's history is greater and older than previously believed. More recently Dr. Schoch has determined the astronomical cause of the demise of antediluvian civilizations, which he describes in his book *Forgotten Civilization: The Role of Solar Outbursts in Our Past and Future* (Inner Traditions, 2012), along with the scientific and archaeological evidence that supports his conclusions.

Dr. Schoch's Website is *www.robertschoch.com.*

Laird Scranton, a software designer from Albany, New York, is the author of two books on African and Egyptian cosmology and language. His focus is on the study of *comparative cosmology,* which is the study of the classic myths, symbols, deities, cosmological concepts, rituals, and words of various ancient and modern cultures.

His emphasis has been on defining fundamental similarities between the cosmologies of the modern-day Dogon tribe of Mali, ancient Egypt, and Buddhism. These studies have culminated in a new symbolic approach to interpreting Egyptian hieroglyphic words that is based on words and definitions drawn from comparative cosmology, rather than the traditional comparative texts of the Rosetta Stone.

His recent studies have extended to the cosmologies and hieroglyphic languages of Tibet and China, with focus on the creation tradition of the priestly Na-Khi tribe. His current book on ancient Chinese cosmology and language, *China's Cosmological Prehistory*, is due out in August 2014 from Inner Traditions.

His articles include three Dogon-related topics in Temple University's forthcoming *Encyclopedia of African Religion* and a recent article in support of Marcel Griaule's Dogon cosmology in the University of Chicago's academic journal *Anthropology News*.

He has been featured in John Anthony West's *Magical Egypt* documentary and Carmen Boulter's *The Pyramid Code*. Links can be found on the internet to radio interviews on Coast to Coast AM in the United Sates and Red Ice Radio in Europe.

Steve Sora was born in New York City and studied history at CW Post on Long Island. His book *Lost Treasure of the Knights Templar*, now in the seventh printing, connects the mystery of the disappearance of the Templar fleet to the Oak Island treasure search. His second book, *Secret Societies of America's Elite*, was released by Inner Traditions in 2003. A third book, *Lost Colony of the Templars*, was released in 2005 and served as strong evidence for the History Channel's "Holy Grail in America." In 2005 *Treasures From Heaven* was released by Wiley & Sons. In 2007 *Triumph of the Sea Gods* was released by Inner Traditions. The author wrote five (of 40) articles for *Forbidden Religion*, edited by J. Douglas Kenyon, and contributed an essay for *Exposed, Uncovered and Declassified, Lost Civilizations and Secrets of the Past* for New Page Books. Steve Sora's books have been reprinted in 12 languages.

The author has been on the *Art Bell Show* and on Whitley Streiber's *Unknown Country*, and on radio shows with Shirley McClaine, Jeff Rense, and Louis Free. He has been on Alex Merklinger's *Mysteries of the Mind*, Debbie Peach's *The Aware Show*, Patte Purcell's *New Dimension*, the *Laura Lee Show*, and the *Dr. Bob Hieronimus Show*. He has appeared in two PAX-TV documentaries and on the DVD liner notes for the Jerry Bruckheimer film *National Treasure*. The Oak Island story was covered for RAI-II (the Italian Discovery Channel) and included the author. Recently *Holy Grail in America* devoted 15 minutes to *Lost Colony of the Templars*. Most recently he appeared in *America Unearthed* with Scott Wolter. The author has more than 200 articles in print on such diverse topics as travel, photography, investing, and non-fiction mystery. Recent articles have appeared in *Atlantis Rising*, where the author is a regular contributor, *Fenix* (Italy), and *Nexus* (Australia). For "The Real War on Troy" he traveled extensively in Portugal, Spain, and Morocco.

He lives in Palmer, Pennsylvania, with his wife, Terry, and his Rottweiler, Jax.

Paul Von Ward, MPA, MSc, interdisciplinary cosmologist, is author of *Children of a Living Universe* (2014), *We've Never Been Alone: A History of Extraterrestrial Intervention* (2011), *The Soul Genome: Science and Reincarnation* (2008), and many other books and articles. With his extensive travels to 100 countries, his wide cultural lens allow him to cope with conflicting worldviews.

For 20 years Paul has focused on explaining evidence of non-human intelligence in our multidimensional universe. His research includes human and nonhuman consciousness and the influence of advanced beings (ABs) on Earth's history. He studies the individual's reactions to human-AB contacts and humanity's place among all extraterrestrial species.

A graduate of Harvard (MPA) and Florida State University (MSc and BA), Paul has served as a Protestant minister; a U.S. naval officer (1962–1965); an American diplomat (1965–1980) in France, Martinique, Sierra Leone, the Dominican Republic, and NATO; and has held senior positions in the U.S. State Department. He was founder/CEO of the Washington-based nonprofit Delphi International Group from 1980 to 1995, an organization that provided international citizen exchanges, professional training, economic development, and Soviet- and Sino-American joint ventures.

Paul's email is paul@vonward.com and his Websites are *www.vonward* *.com* and *www.reincarnationexperiment.org*.

John Richard Ward is an archaeologist, anthropologist, explorer, author, and public speaker from Hereford, England, currently residing in Luxor, Egypt.

Over the last dozen years, he has conducted numerous investigations into ancient Egyptian architecture, culture, religion and its associated symbolism, culminating in various published articles and papers together with scholarly presentations and talks. These investigations have enabled him to carry out assorted explorations of Egypt's vast landscape; from the arid deserts of the Western Sahara to the watery depths of the Hellenistic sunken city of Alexandria, through extreme weather conditions these explorations have provided a wealth of material and archaeological information that contribute to the overall research of ancient Egypt's rich historical past and how attributes of it have been integrated and assimilated within various cultures throughout history. He has also carried out research into the many mysteries surrounding medieval Templarism and its possible connectivity through symbolism to Egyptian antiquity and its clear links to the various esoteric and hermetic cults throughout the ages.

Currently he is a member of the Gebel el Silsila Survey Project team working at the ancient sand stone quarries, the source for many of the ancient upper Egyptian temples.

John lives on the west bank of Luxor, the former location of ancient Thebes, famous today for its ancient historical sites and tombs, with his partner, Dr. Maria Nilsson, their Arabian horses, and a seemingly vast menagerie of animals.